M000159083

THE TOP PERFORMER'S GUIDE TO CHANGE

Essential Skills That Put You On Top

TIM URSINY, PhD AND BARBARA A. KAY, MA

SOURCEBOOKS, INC.
NAPERVILLE, ILLINOIS

Copyright © 2007 by Tim Ursiny and Barbara Kay
Cover and internal design © 2007 by Sourcebooks, Inc.
Cover and internal photo © Digital Vision
Sourcebooks and the colophon are registered trademarks of Sourcebooks, Inc.

Published by Sourcebooks, Inc.
P.O. Box 4410, Naperville, Illinois 60567–4410
(630) 961-3900
Fax: (630) 961-2168
www.sourcebooks.com

Ursiny, Timothy E.
  The top performer's guide to change / Tim Ursiny, Barbara Kay.
     p. cm.
  1. Organizational change. 2. Employees--Attitudes. 3. Attitude change. 4. Success in business. I. Kay, Barbara. II. Title.

HD58.8.U77 2006
658.4'06--dc22

2006012971

Printed and bound in China.
LEO 10 9 8 7 6 5 4 3 2 1

DEDICATION

Tim

To my wife, Marla, the person most responsible for bringing stability and peace to what could have been a very chaotic and messy life.

Barbara

For the love of my life, my greatest supporter, cheerleader, and encourager, who helps me through all life's challenges and celebrates with me all life's successes. To Bob, a fabulous husband and a great man!

CONTENTS

ACKNOWLEDGMENTS

Both authors would like to thank Sourcebooks for their support, guidance, and unerring belief in this project. Our editor, Peter Lynch, is an intelligent and insightful man and we appreciate his help in developing this book so much. We can't say enough about the rest of the crew. Sourcebooks is a company of high energy, dedication, and incredible professionalism. Yet they still are lots of fun to work with! Of course, the publisher Dominique Raccah is a great mentor and friend. This series was truly her brainchild.

We would also like to thank the crew at Advantage Coaching & Training. Carole Smith, Sue Gage, Carole Cowperthwaite-O'Hagan, Antoinette Ayers, and Marc Ybaben are the best people you could possibly hope to work with and they make our days joyful and much easier.

We thank our families for their patience while we were writing this book and we thank our clients for being top performers. We learn so much from you!

INTRODUCTION

We have been working in organizations for many years helping individuals and groups communicate better, build confidence, learn coaching skills, and manage conflict—just about any skill area that is related to human interaction, potential, and performance. Over the last several years we found that requests for workshops dealing with change and transition were growing dramatically.

We had been doing workshops on dealing with change for years and knew that this was a powerful topic for individuals and for corporations. However, we did not suspect the dramatic increase in need for training on this important topic. Change has become the way of the world and people were learning to deal with it or were burning out from feeling bitter and hurt.

A top performer must be a master at dealing with change. Research indicates that poor adaptation to change has many negative consequences for both people and business performance. Mergers are a great example of how poorly most people deal with change. Most studies suggest the 50 percent of all mergers fail. Additionally, only about 20 percent achieve the desired results of the merger. We believe that a large part of the failure is caused by the serious lack of attention to helping people deal with the psychology of change. So much money is invested in merging software systems, manuals, reporting hierarchies, and so on, yet the human element is mostly left to chance. This is deadly for a corporation. Frequently we have been brought in to help when the damage has already been extensive for the workers and the business.

Top performers know that change can be dangerous if dealt with poorly. They also know that change is here to stay and that those who learn skills for dealing with change will have wonderful opportunities. Our purpose for writing this book is to help you seize those opportunities.

To do that we are going to cover important research about change, including the role of perceptions, choices, dangers, and individual differences. We are going to explore how some people get incredibly lucky when going through change while others suffer. Together we will examine how to adjust and thrive during times of change. We will also look beyond your personal growth to help you become a positive leader during times of change. Finally, we will end with a process for helping you develop your own personal change champion strategy. You may feel that the first two sections seem full of background and wonder when you are going to arrive at the how-to's. We hope you hang in and chew on the fundamentals. The how-to comes in the third section and will be much more powerful if you understand potential consequences and opportunities. We believe this background will give you the fuel to energize the how-to's. (Also note that to aid in the flow of reading, we will be using "I" when one of your authors shares a story, regardless of which author it is.)

Top performers know that change is the way of the future. Join this elite group by learning how to swim with the change and arrive at a destination that is far better than you could have ever imagined!

SECTION I

CHALLENGE OF CHANGE

CHAPTER 1

WHY TOP PERFORMERS *MUST* KNOW HOW TO DEAL WITH CHANGE

"Nothing endures but change."
—Heraclitus

How do you feel when something in your life shifts dramatically? People differ greatly when it comes to their reaction to change. Some people love it; they thrive on new opportunities and events. Other people hate the twists and turns of change; they are most content when everything stays the same.

What kind of person are you? Do you roll with the punches pretty well? Do you find that new situations and events bring variety and excitement? Or are you more unsettled by change? Perhaps transitions are difficult and you feel disrupted when your routine is disturbed.

If you don't know, think about how you felt the last time that you were surprised by an announcement of change at work, got a new project, or shifted to another boss. Did you find yourself thinking about the future and new opportunities, or feeling loss or fear over what changed?

Our feelings about change and our styles of interacting with it falls somewhere on a continuum. At the one end are the homesteaders. Homesteaders are the people who like to set down roots and stay in one place. They value consistency and thrive in a steady environment. On the other end are the pioneers. Pioneers feel restless. They like to explore. They travel light and prefer to move on to new places. Homesteaders and pioneers have different challenges and strengths. The United States was built by the positive qualities of both groups. Farms, businesses, and communities would never have been fully developed without the homesteaders. They are responsible for a lot of the enhancements that have been created in our world. At the same time, without the pioneers, we would not have sailed to the "new world," explored past the Appalachian Mountains, crossed the Mississippi River, or climbed over the Rockies. Our pioneers discovered many wonders and opportunities.

Neither group is particularly better or worse, but they do tend to deal with change very differently, each with their own challenges and strengths. Pioneers look for opportunities and are flexible, but tend to get bored when everything stays the same. They sometimes create change when change is not needed. Homesteaders are patient and willing to persevere toward a goal, but struggle because they tend to resist change. Whether you prefer homesteading, pioneering, or something in between, change comes to all of us.

So, what is change? Obviously, change is something that happens, an event. However, change is also the evolution of events. All human history is the story of change. Even the very earth is constantly evolving. Mountains were once plains and deserts were once deep beneath the ocean. The earth takes millions of years to change, but human change happens quickly. And it is happening faster than ever before. When it comes to change, these two things are true: change is inevitable and change is accelerating. Let's look at each more closely.

Change Is Inevitable

When was the last time you had a month where absolutely nothing changed in your life? If you look closely enough you will see that months without change do not exist. Unfortunately, we are in the uncomfortable position of having no control over the existence of change. It is going to happen whether we like it or not. Sure, we can impact on ourselves, our peers, and our circumstances, but we cannot freeze time. Ben Franklin said, "In this world nothing can be said to be certain, except death and taxes." To that we can add change!

Change Is Accelerating

The pace of change is also rapidly accelerating. Technological advances have dramatically increased the speed of our experience. Prior to the industrial age it took months and even years for people and information to travel. In 1804 it took heroic explorers Lewis and Clark two and a half years to travel from St. Louis to the Pacific Ocean and back. Now travel from the Midwest to the West Coast takes only a few hours. Information travels even faster—in mere seconds—across the Internet. Some say we have gained more knowledge in the last century than all the previous centuries combined. The speed of information and the technology that provides rapid production and delivery of goods makes *everyone* as well as *everything* move faster. Change is moving so rapidly that several companies that we work with have spent thousands of dollars to train their people to effectively deal with change. Some are even including questions in the hiring process to gauge how well potential hires deal with change. They know that change is the way of the future and that having workers who struggle with change is a serious danger.

For homesteaders and pioneers alike, constant and rapidly accelerating change is our reality and our future.

Change Is a Process

While change is an inevitable accelerating stream of events, it is also a *process*. The process of change is what people experience in response to events. Experts in business, medicine, and psychology have studied the process of change for decades.

Elizabeth Kubler-Ross was a pioneer in studying this process when she examined the stages of grief in the 1960s. Over the last forty years researchers and academics have further developed Kubler-Ross's theories. Key examples are the work of Dennis O'Connor and Donald Wolfe who in 1987 expanded the theory of change to include "stage of life" transitions. They described a series of five stages:

1) prechange stability

2) rising discontent

3) crisis

4) redirection and adaptation

5) restabilizing

Moving beyond individual changes, in 1990 researchers Dottie Perlman and George Takacs described the experience of organizational change as a process with ten stages.

Now, in just these three examples the change process is described as having anywhere from five to ten stages, and there are many more studies we could describe. Clearly, the information can be more confusing than helpful. Our purpose is to make the academic research accessible and practical. To simplify, the range of research can be summarized in three fundamental change stages: shock, adjustment, and outcome.

Shock

Shock is the first response to the event. All changes bring a shock phase. Sad changes like loss or illness bring shock, and so do happy changes like a new job or promotion. Something has happened to startle us out of our routine. Shock is a natural and normal initial response to this shift.

Adjustment

During the adjustment phase we successfully or unsuccessfully adapt to the new situation. Frequently, we do both as we attempt to adjust our emotions, thinking, and actions to the new reality. This period is filled with conflicting feelings and multiple efforts to regain confidence and stability.

Outcome

Outcome flows from our choices and experiences of shock and adjustment. If we flounder during shock and adjustment, our outcome may be partial recovery or complete stagnation and more instability. However, if we create and pursue successful strategies, the outcome will be positive transformation, top performance, and victory.

Nobody can stop change, but we can influence the results. Some people will march through change, push through obstacles, and move directly toward success. Others will make progress, with struggles and setbacks along the way. Still others will become completely stalled or even regress during times of change.

The process is not fixed, but an outcome is inevitable. The potential outcomes of the change process are shown in Table 1.1.

Negative Outcomes	Positive Outcomes
• Depression	• Enthusiasm
• Anxiety	• Hope
• Withdrawal	• Advancement
• Stagnation	• Growth
• Failure	• Transformation

Table 1.1: Negative and Positive Change Outcomes

Everyone responds differently to the challenge of change. Some stagger and falter and some use it as an opportunity to build and transform. Change will happen, change will require an adjustment process, and change will bring an outcome. Top performers impact the outcomes of change by understanding the process and finding the opportunities. What will be your outcome?

The Tale of Two Outcomes

A portion of our work is with individuals in the financial services arena. We were coaching several financial advisors in 2001 when the stock market took a beating. Our clients (and subsequently their clients) had gotten used to incredible returns on their money, and now they were losing money. Our clients were dealing with lots of change: bad markets, angry clients, and dwindling personal finances.

We want to briefly mention the stories of two of these individuals, Bill and Mike. Both of these gentlemen were very successful in their work, with similar incomes and clientele. Bill, however, was not great at adapting to change. He started avoiding his clients and took a passive "wait and see" stance. When we tried to coach Bill to take a more proactive stance, he started canceling his coaching sessions and even withdrew from us. Mike also had the initial tendency to withdraw, but with some encouragement he started thinking more creatively during this challenging time. He viewed it as a time to build his relationships with his clients as well as pursue new prospects (wisely figuring that many other advisors were avoiding their clients).

Both Bill and Mike struggled for several years, but by early 2005 all of Mike's work paid off. Over time, he dramatically increased the number of high-net-worth clients he served. He also maintained many of his top clients by empathizing with them through their frustrations and serving them as well as he could during the down years. In contrast, Bill lost many of his clients, did no new prospecting, and struggles to this day.

Dealing with negative changes can be difficult for any of us. In chapter 3 we will look more closely at change dangers. However, top performers know how to embrace and work through change to create opportunity and success. As you work through section 3 and the appendix, you will be able to join the ranks of these top performers.

REFLECTION QUESTIONS

The first step to becoming a top performer during times of change is to have insight into yourself. Do the following exercises to increase your knowledge of how you deal with change.

1. Briefly describe a significant change that you have experienced recently.

2. In what way did you handle this change like a homesteader?

3. In what way did you handle this change like a pioneer?

4. In general, what went well in terms of how you dealt with the change?

5. What could have gone even better?

6. What future changes are looming on the horizon?

7. What can you do to be better prepared for future change?

CHAPTER 2

CHANGE CHOICES

"Only I can change my life. No one can do it for me."
—*Carol Burnett*

Change offers us the opportunity for two potential outcomes—we will either experience disappointment or victory. Every time we face change we make choices. Sometimes we make these choices consciously—we decide to push ahead or we decide to wait. Other times, we make disguised decisions by letting the circumstances decide for us (i.e., control us).

Change Victims

Even indecision is a decision. Each time we face change, we make a choice to be either proactive or reactive. The hard truth is that reactive and proactive approaches are not equal choices and they will not create equal outcomes. When we react, we respond as victims rather than top performers. Change victims get trapped in six reactive dead-ends: worry, deny, resist, retreat, blame, and break.

Worry

Worry is a reactive emotional response. It is a natural and understandable response, but it is reactive. To clarify, we must point out that worry is not the same thing as concern. Of course, change brings concern about events and outcomes. Concern is a healthy response and encourages us to act on our own behalf. Worry goes beyond concern. The online website eHealthMD describes worry as "a lasting preoccupation with past or future bad events." The Princeton University dictionary website describes worry as "a strong feeling of anxiety." What makes worry destructive is the nagging nature of constant anxiety. Worry doesn't promote actions or problem solving, it produces fear.

Deny

Some people would rather deny than worry. They ignore the change or convince themselves that the change is not going to affect them. These folks are like the ostrich that puts his head in the sand when trying to hide. The trouble is that the ostrich is in plain sight. In fact, with his head in the sand and his rear end facing the world, the ostrich looks pretty silly and is very vulnerable. When we deny, we are not wasting energy on worry, but we are not spending energy on positive adjustments. This is less painful, but no more productive.

Resist

Resisting is a more conscious form of denying. We are not refusing to *believe* in the change, but we are stubbornly refusing to *adapt*. We have all seen examples of resistance. When companies merge, the workers will often resist forming a united culture. It can become a competition between those from company A's legacy and those from company B's perspective. While the "opposing teams" are fighting over the preferred way of doing things, very little will be accomplished. Worker resistance is a major source of lost productivity during company mergers.

If resisters remain stubborn, other people or circumstances can force an outcome. Company leaders who refuse to adapt will find themselves far behind the competitors. Workers may find themselves stalled in their careers and individuals may struggle even more through stage-of-life transitions. Resisters avoid something they expect to be disagreeable but in return invite an unpredictable and risky outcome.

Retreat

When we retreat, we isolate ourselves from personal and practical resources. Retreaters hole up and don't seek support that would motivate, encourage, and assist their progress.

Some people retreat out of false pride. False pride stems from the fantasy that we are *totally* self-sufficient and *completely* capable of managing *all* events independently. It soothes false pride to act as if we can operate with superhuman competence and independence.

Others retreat out of discouragement or shame. They just don't believe that they are capable of addressing the challenge effectively or are embarrassed by appearing less than competent.

The common denominator between these two types of retreaters is concern about image. We all want to look good in front of others. It is embarrassing to feel that we need help, and retreating diminishes our embarrassment. Top performers know that it takes far more strength and courage to seek support than to retreat.

Blame

Blaming is another reaction of the change victim. Blamers devote all their energy to finger-pointing. They live in the world of "if only": "If only my boss had given clearer instructions, I would not have messed up the presentation," "If only my spouse had made sure my alarm was set, I would not be late for work," "If only my subordinates were more talented, I could please the shareholders."

Blamers push all responsibility away from themselves. The distorted "benefit" of blaming is the false sense of freedom from accountability and action. If we are not responsible, why should we do something about it? Blaming allows us to protect our self-esteem temporarily and may even make us feel superior to others.

This is not to say you can't or shouldn't hold others accountable for mistakes or misconduct. However, a change victim will get *stuck* in blaming, which leads to bitterness and stagnation. A change champion will accept transformation as a personal mission.

Break

To break is to give up or to become completely paralyzed. Breaking can be passive in apathetic immobility or it can be active in self-defeating behaviors. Active breakers will lash out. They will blow up in anger, make rash decisions, or engage in harmful actions. Passive breakers may look like retreaters, but they are different in that retreaters can still work toward progress on their own. Passive breakers will retreat and also become completely immobilized. Active or passive breaking promotes a cycle of disillusionment and self-destruction.

What do you think drives change victims toward these dead ends? No one wakes up in the morning, looks in the mirror, and says, " I think I will make some bad choices and big mistakes today!" What drives a change victim down the dead-end path is their *perceptions* of the change.

Perceptions of Change

In chapter 1 we described change as an event, a process. Change is also a perception. Our perceptions of change may be positive or negative as demonstrated in Table 2.1.

Negative Perceptions	Positive Perceptions
• Change threatens	• Change enhances
• Change confuses	• Change excites
• Change hurts	• Change strengthens
• Change takes	• Change gives
• Change defeats	• Change succeeds

Table 2.1: Negative and Positive Perceptions of Change

Sometimes challenges and changes are not huge life transitions. Sometimes they are just everyday kinds of adventures. I have three boys. The two youngest are twins, but they are total opposites. Like Felix and Oscar from *The Odd Couple*, they approach every situation completely differently. One is cautious and likes routine; he is a homesteader. The other is adventuresome and game for new things; he is a pioneer.

While on vacation some years ago, we decided to teach these boys how to water ski. The homesteader was not keen on this idea. He focused on how frightening it was to be behind this big boat, being pulled along at a high speed. What if he crashed? He was very tense. The pioneer was also quite scared, but he was more game. He focused more on the fun he would have if he actually made it up and went speeding around looking really cool!

As happens, these two had some false starts and some crashes. The homesteader, who was more skilled than the pioneer, got more and more tense and was more concerned about failure after each false start (even though each time he did better). The pioneer also made mistakes (he didn't get up at all or started and then crashed). Overall, the homesteader ended up as the best "almost" water skier. He made it 90 percent of the way up, got scared, and actually let go! Had he held on for two more seconds, he would have been skiing.

What is most important, though, is what happened the next summer. The homesteader remembered all the fear and the times he had not made it up. He was totally focused on what had gone wrong the year before. We kept trying to encourage him by reminding him that he was the very best skier. He wanted none of that. He had a lot of reasons why he did not want to try, mostly revolving around how he really didn't think water skiing would be fun anyway.

In contrast, the pioneer struggled with fear, but along with fear he held the idea of what fun he would have when he succeeded. Over time, the pioneer kept trying and the homesteader continued to stay on the dock. Today the pioneer can ski any time he wants and is proud of being able to water ski. The homesteader has decided that skiing is not for him and stopped trying. Regrettably, the homesteader never got to make the decision based on his real preference, because he focused on his fear. His perception of the situation as being full of danger and risk of failure killed his initiative and courage to keep trying. The pioneer sure did feel fear, but his perception focused on the opportunities and possible success. The image of "cool-dude water skier" kept him going despite the crashes. These boys faced the same circumstances at the same time with very different outcomes. One held on to negative perceptions and the other was able to balance the negatives with the promise of the positives.

Now, this does *not* mean that homesteaders always quit and pioneers always succeed in change. In fact, my homesteader succeeds fabulously because like many homesteaders he is conscientious and willing to work toward a goal. If my homesteader had perceived the situation differently, he would be a great water skier.

For each of us there are numerous challenges when it comes to change. One of those challenges is perception. We have a choice: we can focus on the negatives or we can focus on the positives. If we spend all our energy thinking about the negatives, we are much more likely to fall into the change victim patterns of worry, deny, resist, retreat, blame, or break. We can choose to become a change victim or a top-performing change champion. We can overcome instead of succumb.

Top performers know six conquering disciplines that we will mention here briefly and expand upon in detail in later chapters.

1. Grieve

Grieving is critical! No one walks away from significant change unscathed. Grieving is a real and necessary part of becoming a change champion.

2. Accept

Accepting encourages healthy grief and moving forward. When we accept, we face the music. We know that there are things beyond our control and that we must work to adjust ourselves to the situation.

3. Plan

Accepting leads to planning. When we accept the challenge, we desire to overcome the hurdles and achieve success. Change champions spend energy making plans that will help them triumph.

4. Act

Change champions follow their plans with action. Roadblocks do not bog them down. They continue to move forward, adjusting their plans with new strategies as the circumstances require.

5. Forgive

The opposite of blaming is forgiving. Forgiving is a freeing and grace-giving exercise. Forgiveness liberates us as much as the offender.

6. Build

To build means that we work step-by-step to create a new reality. Building includes acquiring knowledge, resources, skills, and people who can contribute to the cause. Top performers act like a general contractor. They will do what they can do, get help for what they can't do, and stay on top of the project until completion.

REFLECTION QUESTIONS

Let's examine some of your past change choices.

1. Name a past change that you chose to deal with utilizing one of the following choices: worry, deny, resist, retreat, blame, or break.
   - Why do you think you made this choice?
   - How well did this choice serve you?
   - What would have been a better choice in dealing with this change?
   - What was the outcome of making these choices?
2. Name a past change in which you were able to do some or all of the following: grieve, accept, plan, act, forgive, or build.
   - Why do you think you made this choice?
   - How well did this choice serve you?
   - What was the outcome of choosing to deal with the change in this way?

SECTION II
SURVIVING CHANGE

CHAPTER 3

CHANGE DANGERS

"Change is the constant, the signal for rebirth, the egg of the Phoenix."
—*Christina Baldwin*

In the last chapter we spoke of the inevitable choice that each of us must make when faced with change. In this chapter we will examine the threats, fears, and dangers that have an impact on our choices in the change process. Objectively the choices are simple. If we were purely logical, we would always make the most productive choice. However, humans are not just logical calculators, nor do we want to be.

In the futuristic film *I-Robot*, actor Will Smith distrusts the robot assistants that are a household fixture in the futuristic society. The film depicts a traffic accident during which Smith's car and another car plunge into the Chicago River. Both cars sink fast and water fills the passenger compartments. Two survivors are in the river, Will Smith in his car and a child passenger in the other car. A robot jumps in after the cars. It calculates that only one rescue can succeed and determines that Will has the stronger likelihood of surviving. While screaming at the robot to save the other person, Will Smith is rescued and the other survivor is left to drown. Will never trusts a robot again. The robot let a child die.

Logically the robot may have been right, but from an emotional perspective, the loss of a child is the greater tragedy. It is our feelings that make us human. We are blessed and cursed as creatures with both heavenly and beastly feelings. Our highest emotions call us to give, sacrifice, create, and love. Our basest impulses arise from a more primitive place. They arise from fear. Fear lives in a place in our brains called the amygdala. The amygdala is located at the base of the temporal lobe just forward of the brain stem and is the source of primitive human emotions. The amygdala doesn't think; it reacts, often with fear.

The Primal Fear of Change

Fear is the most basic human emotion. It is necessary for survival. Humans would not have survived in the primitive world without fear as a tool to escape danger. Fear triggers our body to fight or flee. Sometimes fighting or fleeing is the healthy protective response. If we are physically threatened by danger, the amygdala is right on target. However, the amygdala does not lay dormant until extreme danger appears. Like a wild beast, it prowls around our brains ready to strike at any opportunity. It pounces when our most primitive needs are threatened, even if we are not in real danger. For example, a company merger can unleash insecurity that far exceeds the actual risks. We often exaggerate the real danger of such a change. Top performers know that these exaggerated dangers need to be thought through logically and dealt with strategically.

The famous psychologist Abraham Maslow (1908–1970) illustrated human needs in his famous Hierarchy of Needs pyramid. The lowest level of the pyramid holds our most basic needs. These include food, shelter, and safety. On the top of the pyramid rests our less-essential needs including self-actualization. Maslow determined that our needs were met from the bottom up. Only after we satisfy our basic needs can we expend energy on higher-order desires. For example, self-actualization is not possible while we are struggling to acquire food, shelter, and safety.

If any of the needs in our pyramid are threatened, fear is aroused. Dan Baker, author of *What Happy People Know*, describes two primal fears: fear of not *having* enough and fear of not *being* enough. The fear of not having enough is connected to our physical needs like food, shelter, and comfort. The fear of not being enough is connected to our fundamental psychological well-being—our fear of failing, being alone, and being rejected. These are summarized in Table 3.1.

Physical Threats	Psychological Threats
Not enough:	Fear of:
• Food	• Failure
• Shelter	• Isolation
• Comfort	• Rejection

Table 3.1: Physical and Psychological Fears

During times of change, the twin fear beasts of not having and not being enough rear their ugly heads. These prowlers sense danger and start scanning the landscape for physical and psychological threats related to the change. While change *circumstances* are different, five change *fears* are common to all situations. During times of change, our basic security and sense of well-being is threatened. Normality and stability are disrupted. It is a natural, even biological, response to feel fear. Out of the amygdala arise five common change fears.

Common Change Fears

• Change fear #1: *I don't know what will happen!*

Everyone feels this fear. The ancient and continuing practices of fortune telling, astrology, and tarot-card reading address this fear. We feel better when we believe that we have a way of gaining a sense of the future (even the impression of knowing the future makes us feel better). Unfortunately, for the most part, we are forced on a journey with no road map and it feels dreadfully scary.

• Change fear #2: *I don't know how to act!*

For every life change you can find a how-to book. Some come with built-in orientation programs. Most companies offer some form of an orientation program. Hospitals routinely offer how-to training for new parents, and houses of worship offer marriage preparation for newly engaged couples. We all want to know how to act. During change we fear that we will not know what to do.

• Change fear #3: *I will lose things!*

Sometimes during change we lose things of value. When people actually lose possessions, jobs, or even family members, then the losses are profound and real. However, the fear we are discussing here is not about these real losses. Instead we are talking about the fear that we *might* lose things. Think about the last time you felt exaggerated fear. Perhaps you were called to a meeting and assumed the worst possible scenario. Or your boss or coworker sent you a curt message and you exaggerated their curtness as evidence of a looming conflict or loss. We can imagine all kinds of *potential* losses, and some people drive themselves crazy with these "what if" scenarios during times of change.

• Change fear #4: *I won't have skills!*
Whenever we face change, unidentified challenges arise and we can fear failure. During our more primitive days we routinely faced perilous trials. Being unprepared could mean deprivation, harm, or death. Thankfully, present change does not usually carry such extreme threat. However, the amygdala does not know the difference. The alarm that served us well in a more primitive world can now be a disadvantage. Often we blow a setback up to be a devastating and life-threatening situation when in truth it is merely a hardship, challenge, or learning experience. Notice how people react during times of lay-off. While you can certainly empathize with a certain level of concern, intense fear does not help solve the problem. People in this situation need enough fear to mobilize and focus on the skills they do have. They can either become invaluable to the company or seek a new job. Intense fear of not having the skills can keep them from acting productively and effectively to regain stability.

- Change fear #5: *I will lose relationships!*

Being rejected or alone is a fundamental fear. During change we fear the loss of connections with other people. This is part of the reason why *prolonged* corporate layoffs are particularly painful. Who will stay and who will go? Will I be able to maintain my relationships if I lose my job? In fact, separation is so painful that people often unintentionally break bonds before a planned departure. For example, employees who face retirement or a planned move may find themselves withdrawing long before their departure date. They might even find that they no longer wish to socialize as they did in the past. Being irritable and finding fault with others is common. This is an unconscious effort to lessen the separation pain and feel some false sense of control over the loss. It is easier to leave folks we find annoying than folks we are going to miss.

During change, these five fears act like a pack of wolves circling around us. They prey on our minds, pounce on our bodies, and drive us to quiver, resist, or flee. Remember, these fears live in our primitive brain. They push us to react and are irrational. If we listen to the fears, they will promote dangerous misperceptions.

Four Paralyzing Perceptions

Psychologist Martin Seligman discovered the power of perception on behavior in his classic learned helplessness experiment. He placed dogs in a cage and restrained them. Next, he gave them an electrical shock from which they could not escape because of a restraint. (This experiment was conducted in 1965 when animal protections were not as advanced.) Next, he placed the same dogs unrestrained in a double cage with a low barrier between the two sides and shocked them again. He fully expected the dogs to jump the barrier into the second cage and escape the shock. To his surprise the dogs lay there and took the shock. Lastly, a new group of dogs (that had never been shocked or restrained) were placed in the double cage. They quickly jumped the barrier when shocked and avoided further pain. Seligman discovered that the first group of dogs "learned" to be helpless. When these dogs were shocked repeatedly without any possibility of escape, they stopped trying to improve their situation and tolerated the pain. When these same dogs were placed in a new situation where they could easily avoid the shock, they still sat there! Even though escape was easy, the dogs continued their self-defeating habit of sitting instead of moving.

The dog's *perception* that pain was unavoidable prevented them from making an easy escape. That perception was so unshakable and pervasive that the dogs did not recognize a positive opportunity when it was directly in front of them. Perception is a powerful force. People's actions are driven by their perceptions. If you perceive yourself to be capable and the situation to be manageable (or even an opportunity) you will act very differently than if you perceive yourself to be helpless and the situation to be hopeless. Just like the dogs, people can be trapped by negative perceptions. There are four paralyzing perceptions that stop us in our tracks.

1. This is forever!
When we are in a difficult situation, it is easy to slip into thinking the difficulties will last forever. This is especially true when someone has experienced a series of changes. One client I worked with had reported to five different managers in the period of nineteen months. She didn't believe that she would *ever* have a permanent manager. Some people experience several job losses in a row. It is

not uncommon for such workers to lose confidence in their ability to ever get a job. Whether it is multiple layoffs, several downturns in the business, or years of chaotic performance in the stock market, we often think that what is happening today will happen forever. *Forever* can be an overwhelming perception.

2. There is nothing I can do!
Another helpless perception is the feeling that we have no control. The dogs in the experiment suffered from this "thinking." In reality, there was an easy solution. Their perception, not reality, prevented them from moving. The perception of no control can make us lie down like dogs when we could be moving toward solutions. Like we mentioned previously, many of our financial services clients experienced this feeling of helplessness after the stock market shifted downward in March of 2001. They quit calling their clients because they felt helpless to make them money and were also fearful of angry clients who had lost significant funds. These financial advisors (like Bill from our previous story) fared poorly during this time. Others we worked with (like Mike), however, used this time to strengthen personal relationships with clients, walk through their losses with them, and even start marketing to clients who were being ignored by their advisors. These individuals have rebuilt their businesses and are thriving.

3. This is entirely my fault!
The opposite of the perception of no control is excessive self-blame. It is equally immobilizing. Like the dogs in Seligman's experiments, self-blame prevents people from gaining relief. People who are laid off during a downsizing may feel completely

responsible for their job loss. The reason for being laid off may have nothing to do with performance or the person's characteristics. The same can occur with the individual who has a change in responsibilities and now has fewer direct reports. While the change may have been made for purely organizational reasons, the person may falsely blame him or herself. Unfortunately even when change decisions have nothing to do with the person's performance, some people still blame themselves. Excessive self-blame prevents us from acting for our own benefit.

4. This is everywhere!
The twin of "forever" is "everywhere." This perception fools us into believing that the same problems affect every area of our lives. When someone goes through stress at home they often start seeing similar challenges at work. A struggle on the home front might spill over to make work also feel like a struggle. Because of the negative mindset, they may actually create situations that cause all areas of their life to go badly. We have been brought into corporations a number of times because a good producer slid into negativity and diminished performance. Many times this was related to a problem outside of work, but the person had not learned to compartmentalize the stress and perceived the difficulties as universal. The pervasive misperception of "everywhere" can make us prisoners of circumstances.

Just reviewing these paralyzing perceptions is depressing! Thinking them and living them is completely counterproductive. The famous philosopher René Descartes stated, "I think; therefore *I am.*" An expansion of this truism is "I think; therefore *I do.*" Top performers do not spontaneously develop. They discipline themselves to become self-aware. They examine their perceptions and

[31]

their feelings. Top performers know that what we think will dictate what we do. The four paralyzing *perceptions* of "forever," "nothing I can do," "entirely me," and "everywhere" lead to *actions* that sabotage our productivity, adjustment, and progress. We call these actions the Sabotaging S's.

The Sabotaging S's

The Sabotaging S's combine all the change victim patterns from chapter 2 (worry, deny, resist, retreat, blame, and break) into three easy-to-remember concepts:

1. **Stick**
2. **Sink**
3. **Shove**

Stick

The first Sabotaging S is *stick*. When we stick, we stay rigid in perception, position, and performance. We can stick in a place of blame or victimhood. When we stick in blame, we have taken on the "nothing I can do" perception. It has nothing to do with us and we have no control over the situation. We become critical and angry. All our energy is focused on complaining and blaming.

A sad example of this is the media coverage of Hurricane Katrina on the Gulf Coast. Immediately following the disaster, the media focused its broadcasting on local, state, and national political representatives blaming others for lack of responsiveness. Some public figures made accusations of willful neglect. The horror of the natural disaster was increased by blame. The victims so burdened by loss were further demoralized by the allegation of intentional abandonment. Equally sad, the heroic efforts of countless first responders were undermined and devalued by the constant blaming. One Chicago-area pilot (who was a helicopter rescuer) said that he felt like he was back in the Vietnam era. After risking his life, the only news coverage was blaming and critical. Blaming accomplishes nothing and increases the negative impact of change. While this is a dramatic example, we can easily look in the workplace and find frequent blame and finger-pointing. We feel better when we can blame someone else for our challenges, but this does not lead to a top-performing mindset.

We can also stick in victimhood. A victim is paralyzed by the perception of no control, and the response is more self-focused than other-focused. It is the "poor me" syndrome. The *Peanuts* cartoon character Charlie Brown is a humorous example. Everything is always going wrong for Charlie Brown. He even makes sure that it goes wrong by predicting that it will. Psychologists call this a self-fulfilling prophecy. Victims also take on the "entirely me" perception. They have no confidence that they will be able to make a positive impact. The *Peanuts* cartoon strip has great illustrations of both the victim and the blamer. Charlie Brown is the defeated victim and his cartoon colleague Lucy is the chronic blamer. When you are not in a top-performing mode, which role is a temptation for you? Are you tempted to be Charlie Brown or Lucy?

Sink

Sink is the second Sabotaging S. When we sink, we fall into self-destructive actions. Sink can arise from any of the four negative perceptions. Sink behaviors include utilizing substances or escapist activities to suspend distress. Alcohol, drugs (legal and illegal), caffeine, food, excessive sleep, and overdependence on television/video games/Internet are common distractions.

Now, not all recreation is dangerous. Top performers know that it is important to have respite from chronic stress. It is healthy for us to take intentional breaks. However, these breaks need to be part of productive recuperation, not an escape that promotes dependency. Top performers use positive self-care to maximize performance, not to escape from their perceived reality.

Shove

Sink and *stick* are often accompanied by their cousin *shove*. Shove can also be related to any of the four negative perceptions. It happens when we push away all helpful support and resources. Sometimes we shove out of depression. Sometimes we shove out of a false pride. Whatever the motivation, the effect is the same. We attempt to stand alone.

Returning to our discussion of Hurricane Katrina, we see an example of a rescue story that illustrates the futility of shove. Ted Koppel entered New Orleans shortly after the hurricane to anchor *Nightline* live from the devastated area. Most of the population had been successfully evacuated except for the few individuals who refused to leave, including Rose. Rose and her husband were elderly and lived in a severely flooded area of town. Water had risen up to their raised porch, leaving just enough room to get out the front door. They had no electricity, no running water, no sanitation, no air conditioning, and limited food. The floodwaters were polluted with waste, chemicals, and decay, creating a toxic stew. It was an unbearable environment. Their adult daughter was begging them to leave but Rose did not want to leave her house; she seemed afflicted with shove! Ted Koppel floated to her doorstep with the *Nightline* news crew. Even the famous news reporter could not convince her to leave. Finally after a long period of coaxing, Rose accepted help and was "rescued."

But Rose is not unique in this. We all can get trapped in perceptions and behaviors that do not serve us. When you go through great changes and difficulties, do you tap into the power of your friendships and community or do you isolate yourself from help and support? Top performers do not get sidetracked by stick, sink, or shove. They rally themselves, their resources, and their allies to overcome challenges and create a winning outcome.

Not All Took the Shock

As we move forward, it is important to point out one more fact about the Seligman's experiment: most but not all the dogs that had been restrained took the punishment. About one third of them escaped. They persisted and won!

We can keep trying too! Even the most successful people get knocked down. William Avery Bishop was the top Canadian fighter pilot in WWI, but he didn't start out that way. As a poor student, he barely made it through military college. He tried to get into flight school but had to remain an observer because the Canadian air force had their limit of pilots. Hanging on, he finally was able to attend flight school only to be stalled by lack of natural talent. Determined to earn his wings, he practiced hours beyond the required flight-school training. However, his clumsy style caused a crash during the war and almost grounded him. Unwavering in his pursuit to redeem himself, Bishop rebounded the next day to chase a German plane into a nine thousand-foot dive right into the ground. Ultimately, his determination overcame his lack of natural talent and made him one of the best fighter pilots in the world. He was awarded Britain's highest honor, the Victoria Cross.

Often we make the mistake of thinking that circumstances or special talents determine our success during times of change. This perception places us in a helpless position. Bishop could have been defeated by failures and developed a perception of the situation as insurmountable and himself as incompetent. Instead, he used perception to his advantage. He perceived opportunities for success and himself as capable of achieving. Bishop was not a top talent, but he was a top performer. We have the same opportunity. We can use powerful perceptions to drive our determination to become top performers during change.

REFLECTION QUESTIONS

Let's examine the four paralyzing perceptions in more detail. Think about a time in your life when you did not handle change well. Then use the list below to rate, on a scale of 1 to 5, how well each statement represents your perception of the event at the time.

"At the time, I thought that the change would last forever"

1	2	3	4	5
I didn't believe this	Mildly believed	Unsure	Strongly believed	100% believed this

"At the time, I thought there was nothing that I could do about it"

1	2	3	4	5
I didn't believe this	Mildly believed	Unsure	Strongly believed	100% believed this

"At the time, I thought it was about me (I personalized it)"

1	2	3	4	5
I didn't believe this	Mildly believed	Unsure	Strongly believed	100% believed this

"At the time, I thought that the change would impact every area of my life"

1	2	3	4	5
I didn't believe this	Mildly believed	Unsure	Strongly believed	100% believed this

Now, with the benefit of hindsight in your corner, answer the following questions concerning that same event:

1. To what degree did the difficulties endured during this change last forever?

2. What was one behavior that you could have done that might have had some impact on the situation?

3. Was the change personal and entirely about you or were there other factors or people involved?

4. In hindsight, was the change everywhere? What areas of your life did the change not affect?

Exercise

Apply the insights gained from examining this past change to some current challenge you are enduring. Find a way to see the event as temporary, isolated to certain areas of your life, and not personal. Then look at what behaviors and attitudes are in your control and focus on these to build your confidence and performance.

CHAPTER 4

INCREASING YOUR LUCK DURING TIMES OF CHANGE

"I'm a great believer in luck, and I find the harder I work the more I have of it."
—*Thomas Jefferson*

In the last chapter we uncovered personal paralyzing *perceptions* and sabotaging *actions* that profoundly impact our ability to adapt during change. But how do external circumstances impact our overall success? What is the role of luck? Aren't some folks just blessed with good luck? Change often seems to work out positively for them! It would be easy to be confident during times of change if you were as lucky as some individuals.

Studies on Luck

The beautiful thing about modern science is we study just about everything—even luck! British psychologist Richard Wiseman is a leading expert on luck. In 1994, he started the Luck Project to find out if lucky people were born or made. During his extensive research he discovered a critical fact. Lucky people act and think differently than unlucky people! Lucky people share a common pattern of actions and attitudes. Unlucky people also share commonalities. The two patterns are very different.

People who believe they are lucky have a distinct set of expectations and behaviors. They are generally relaxed, optimistic, and open-minded. They also seek variety, hunt for opportunities, and view challenges positively. Conversely, people who consider themselves unlucky tend to be anxious, fearful, and narrowly focused. They avoid variety and tend to miss opportunities.

Lucky People	Unlucky People
• Relaxed	• Anxious
• Optimistic	• Fearful
• Open-Minded	• Narrowly Focused
• Seek Variety	• Avoid Variety
• Seek Opportunities	• Miss Opportunities
• Make Lemonade	• Expect the Worst

People make their own luck! The anxiety, pessimism, and narrow focus of unlucky people prevent them from gaining opportunities. How does this happen? Harvesting apples is a good illustration. Imagine that your job is to harvest as many apples as possible. If you enter the apple orchard anxious and pessimistic, you will have limited energy for finding apples. Further, if you keep a narrow focus, perhaps only looking on the ground, you will find few apples. Even more, if you circle around the same area, you will pick up all the apples in your small circle and ultimately find no more.

Expect Success

Harvesting apples is like gathering opportunities. Lucky people are more successful because they do it differently. They are filled with optimistic energy and they open their eyes to all possibilities. They expect to be successful and they search the entire orchard—even adjoining orchards—for fruit. Ultimately, their open expectations and wide search produce bushels of opportunities.

Barnett Helzberg Jr. is man who loaded a bushel basket with apples by being open and ready. Barnett is a good businessman who built up a chain of highly successful jewelry stores with annual revenue of $300 million. At sixty he was beginning to think about his next stage of life. One day, as he was walking down a New York City street, he heard a woman near the Plaza Hotel call out, "Mr. Buffet!" Barnett wondered: could this possibly be *the* Mr. Buffet, one of the wealthiest men in America?

Barnett had read how Warren Buffet decides to make acquisitions for his conglomerate and thought that his company might be a prime candidate. Barnett turned, walked right up to the gentleman, and introduced himself. Lucky Barnett! The man on the street turned out to be *the* Mr. Warren Buffet. One year later, Buffet purchased Helzberg jewelry stores. Like many lucky people, Barnett Helzberg was open to opportunity, looking for connections, and bold in seizing the moment. He did not stop to think about possible embarrassment or whether his company was worth pursuing by such a huge tycoon. He went for it and luck was made!

In fact, Wiseman's research has shown that people could be trained to be lucky. One company trained in luck showed sales increases of 20 percent each month with the final month being the strongest performance in three years.

Train to Be Lucky

Training has a big impact, for good or for ill! People can be trained to be lucky. Conversely, Seligman's work showed us that we can also be trained to be helpless. Interestingly (as noted at the end of the last chapter) some of the dogs in Seligman's experiments kept trying and leapt away from the shock. How did one-third of the dogs overcome their helplessness training? It turns out that many of the successful dogs came from the pound. The helpless training did not take because these dogs built a reserve of skill from past challenges. They had earlier trained to overcome hardships and were able to draw on that to succeed.

We have the same opportunity. Although it may seem crazy, disruption can be good. We can use times of change to train for current and future success. In fact, the experts have a name for this. It is called *psychological immunity*. Let's look at how this mindset is created.

Creating Psychological Immunity

Psychological immunity has four components:

• Immunization
Experiencing distress in the here and now builds emotional protection for the future. Current pain makes us less sensitive to future pain. Regardless of the outcome, we can be less distressed the next time. No challenge is wasted—each situation builds durability if we allow it.

• Rebound
If we build skills on dealing with change and stress while we are going through the challenges, we bounce back faster each time. It's just like launching an exercise routine. The first phase of any regime is the most painful. We are sore and tired for a long time. Yet as we continue, we are able to exert ourselves more fully and able to recover quickly. Training for change not only decreases pain, it also increases the speed of recovery.

• Hardiness
Training also builds strength. The more we train, the more we can handle difficulties with ease. If you know someone who has run a marathon, you know they train for months, even years. No one runs 26.2 miles on a whim. As they train, they build incredible stamina. Soon, runs that would challenge the average athlete are a piece of cake. Change training operates much the same. Each success builds stamina to overcome new challenges in the future.

• Adaptability
Finally, training for change increases our mental adaptability. We are more successful at adjusting to events and creating a mental map that helps us navigate through the circumstances. We more quickly adjust our expectations to deal with realities on the ground, which in turn speeds our success.

The bonus for change training is that it increases both present and future success. Top performers know that becoming a change champion is a win-win situation (as demonstrated in Table 4.1).

Present Benefits	Future Benefits
1. Succeed Now	1. Bigger Successes
2. Feel Better	2. Easier, Less Distress
3. Gain Confidence	3. Greater Confidence
4. Add Skills	4. More Adept
5. Create Opportunity	5. Increased Openness
6. Increase Strength	6. More Resilient

Table 4.1: Benefits of Becoming a Change Champion

The political biography of Margaret Thatcher is a fine example. Margaret Thatcher ultimately became the first female prime minister of the United Kingdom. However, most of her training came during times of party challenges. She was elected to Parliament in 1959 while her Conservative Party was the ruling party of the British government. By 1964 the Conservatives were defeated and Thatcher and her party were out of power. The Conservatives gained power again for a short time beginning in 1970. In 1974 they were ousted again and remained out of power until 1979.

While in the political backseat, Thatcher worked to develop vital knowledge and skills. As part of the "loyal opposition" she broadened her experience in national affairs. She also wrote articles for the *Daily Telegraph* defending her political ideals.

In a surprise power shuffle, Thatcher seized an opportunity and became the Conservative Party leader in 1975. During her time as leader of the losing party, she expanded her education to international policy by visiting nations around the world. Finally, when the British ousted the Labour Party in 1979, she became prime minister. Her preparation during her party's weak period paved the way for her long-term success. She became a powerful leader nationally and internationally, holding the office of prime minister for more than twenty years.

Thatcher could have given up when her party was repeatedly stuck in a powerless position. She could have learned to be helpless. Instead she used that time of challenge to build skills and resilience. She also made her own luck by seizing opportunity when it came. Her training in overcoming challenge and seizing opportunity paid off big time! Not only was she the first female prime minister of

Britain, but also she held power for longer than any British leader in the twentieth century.

We have the same choice as Thatcher. We can train for success or we can let circumstances train us for helplessness. We will certainly learn some pattern. It can be a pattern of unlucky helplessness or a pattern of lucky thriving. It is all matter of choice! Top performers do not wait for change and hope for the best. They prepare themselves for the challenges and therefore excel through difficulties while others flounder. In section 3 we will explore how to build your skills and train for change. How do you want to train for change?

REFLECTION QUESTIONS

1. When was the last time that you felt really lucky?

   • What did you believe or feel at the time that might have aided your luck?

   • What actions did you take that may have increased your luck?

2. Think of a situation that you are avoiding that could possibly create some great opportunity for you. What step could you take toward opportunity with this situation?

3. How might you apply the concepts of immunization, rebound, hardiness, and adaptability to train yourself in building psychological immunity to the effects of change?

SECTION III
THRIVING IN CHANGE

CHAPTER 5

ADAPTING TO CHANGE

"They always say time changes things, but you actually have to change them yourself."
—*Andy Warhol*

In the first two sections we discussed the inevitability of change and the increased pace of change. We also have discussed change as a process as well as an event. Finally, we reviewed the positive and negative choices that decide the ultimate outcome of the change process.

The Impact of Personal Style

There is an additional area we need to address before moving forward, and that is how personal style affects your dealings with change. We have found that it is profoundly helpful in a variety of situations to understand your personal style and develop skills in adapting to others' personal styles.

Understanding variations in personal style is an important tool in becoming a change champion. Gone are the days when we expected all people to act and react the same. Early industrialists thought mechanized manufacturing and treating people like interchangeable parts was great. Over time we found that this approach kills the human spirit, destroys creativity, and reduces effectiveness. We now understand that people need to be treated as individuals. Individual reactions to change vary and these reactions can help or hurt our change success. Understanding personal style will enable us to strategize effectively in order to reduce our limitations and leverage our strengths.

It is important to note that personal style is *not* the same thing as personality. Our personality is a set of fixed characteristics that do not change over time. There are some good tests that evaluate personality. The California Personality Inventory is one. It has several hundred questions and is well regarded in the psychology field as a good measure of stable personality traits. Fortunately, we are not attempting to unlock core personality, so thankfully we are spared a lengthy test!

We are interested in personal style. Personal style is how we interact in different environments and with different people. It is influenced by our core personality, but it is more adaptable. A metaphor for the difference between personality and personal style is the comparison of our bodies with our clothes. Our core personalities are like our bodies. For the most part, our bodies don't change. We wake up to the same limbs, hands, feet, and face from the day before. Our personal style is like our clothes. They change dramatically based on needs for the moment. We wear a completely different outfit to the beach than to a black-tie event. The same body is underneath the clothes, but we change our exterior to match the situation.

The idea of personal styles was explored by psychologist William Marston when he studied the emotions of normal people in the early part of the twentieth century. Since his groundbreaking work, further work has been conducted and excellent assessments have been developed that identify personal styles. We have found that different assessments based on Marston's work use slightly different words to describe the same concepts. We happen to use the DiSC® Model developed by Inscape Publishing.

DiSC describes four main personal styles: Dominance, Influence, Steadiness, and Conscientiousness. An easy way to identify the four styles is to understand the two continuums that are the basis of the DiSC Model—*approach* and *focus of attention.* The approach continuum is how an individual interacts in a given situation. People have a tendency to prefer an approach that is either more *spontaneous* or more *methodical.* Those who prefer a *spontaneous* approach tend to think quickly, act quickly, and are extroverted and confident with others. Those who prefer a *methodical* approach tend to take time to evaluate, are cautious in acting, and are more reserved in their expressions.

The second continuum is focus of attention. Those who focus on tasks are on one end of the continuum. Those who focus on relationships are on the other end of this continuum. When people are task-focused they are interested in products and results. As they encounter a situation they usually think more about the tasks to be completed than the individuals involved. Those who focus on relationships are more engaged with the people involved in the tasks than the to-do list. By combining continuums—approach (spontaneous or methodical) and focus of attention (tasks or relationships)—we arrive at four main behavior styles: Dominance, Influence, Steadiness, and Conscientiousness.

	Spontaneous Approach	Methodical Approach
Task Focus	Dominance	Conscientiousness
Relationship Focus	Influence	Steadiness

- The *Dominance* style has a spontaneous approach and task focus. Individuals who show a dominance style are movers and shakers. They tend to be results-oriented, independent, and confident and like to make decisions quickly. If dominance had a motto it would be "Just do it."

- The second style, *Influence*, also has a spontaneous approach, but is more focused on relationships than on tasks. Individuals who exhibit the influence style tend to be enthusiastic, charismatic, and fun. They are often motivated by recognition, interaction, and freedom from details. Influence's motto might be "Let's have fun, let's be inspired."

- *Steadiness*, like Influence, has a people focus. But it has a methodical rather than a spontaneous approach. Steadiness individuals tend to be loyal, cooperative, calm, and stable. They are caring and diplomatic. They prefer to work behind the scenes instead of in the spotlight. They value security, stability, cooperation, and sincere appreciation. The motto for steadiness would likely be "Let's get along, let's work together."

- The last of the four styles is *Conscientiousness*. Conscientiousness individuals exhibit a task focus like Dominance, but a methodical approach like Steadiness. Conscientiousness individuals tend to be analytical and precise. They highly value quality and accuracy. They are often motivated by known standards, defined expectations, and quality. If conscientiousness had a motto it would be "Do it right."

We have all met folks who exhibit these styles in different ways. You likely recognize these styles in your own work setting or circle of friends. The following paints a light-hearted picture of how these styles might differ in an everyday setting:

You are with a large group of people waiting for an elevator and the doors finally open up.

- If you are high in Dominance, you step into the elevator and push the "close door" button.
- If you are high in Influence, you step in the elevator and say, "Come on, there's room for everyone!"
- If you are high in Steadiness, you let everyone step in and wait for the next elevator.
- If you are high in Conscientiousness, you step in, size up everyone, and then look at the weight limit charts on the elevator to ensure you will make it to the top.

The elevator scenario helps depict the styles in a simple way. But it would be a mistake to label others or ourselves as purely D, i, S, or C. First, we must remember that personal style is not personality. Personal style is adaptable and it does not classify us. Second, each of us displays various combinations of the four styles. This mixture also shifts as we change situations, just like we change clothes based on circumstances. This variety of mixtures is what makes us all unique and what makes understanding personal style powerful. If we develop a better understanding of our preferences in given situations and learn how to adapt, we can be more effective and successful.

Even though we have a mixture of the four styles and can shift, we usually have primary and secondary preferences in our routine environments. When our clients take the DiSC Classic profile, we ask them to focus their answers on the setting that they are evaluating. For most, it is the work environment. At work, we usually develop a pattern that is most comfortable for us. We call this the default style. Our default style is based on our preferences, roles, relationships, and interactions. Based on what we have described thus far, you may have a good idea of your style preferences at work.

How the Different Styles Deal with Change

Obviously, these four styles will have very different ways of approaching change. Top performers who are high in Dominance will likely want to take charge during change. They may rapidly shift their thinking, pick a new course of action, and appreciate the challenge of overcoming new obstacles. Top performers who are high in Influence may embrace the adventure and variety provided by change. They will look for a way to be inspired and inspire others during the process. Top performers who are high in Steadiness may want to focus on the things that will remain stable. They may look for and give support to those around them to help keep the team together. Top performers who are high in Conscientiousness may analyze the change and look for ways that they can maintain quality. They will do their homework and make careful plans to navigate the new territory.

The good news is that there is no best style. All of the styles have strengths and challenges. No style will automatically succeed more than the others. Style awareness and adaptability are far more critical to success than a particular style preference. Understanding the unique strengths and challenges for each style during a time of change enables us to maximize strengths and minimize limitations.

The following chart highlights key gifts and gaps:

	Gifts	Gaps
Dominance	• Proactive	• Dislikes loss of control
	• Decisive	• Frustrated by delay
	• Likes challenge	• May fight
	• Independent	• May reject help
Influence	• Likes variety	• Easily distracted
	• Inspiring	• Needs affirmation
	• Flexible	• May overlook details
	• Positive	• May overlook risks
Steadiness	• Steady	• May resist change
	• Diplomatic	• May avoid conflict
	• Accommodating	• May give in
	• Cautious	• May be slow in responding
Conscientiousness	• Analytical	• May get stuck in planning
	• Cautious	• May miss opportunities
	• Objective	• May appear disengaged
	• Precise	• May expect perfection

Those who understand their own style and can adapt to the styles of others are the most successful, productive, and effective. There are important steps that can be taken to create more balance and effectiveness for each style preference. We will go through each as it relates to being a change champion.

Dominance

Challenges—Those who exhibit high dominance tend to be directive and assertive and are most comfortable when they have control. Change often brings circumstances beyond our control. The aggravation caused by loss of control turns up the volume on the Dominance style. Assertive can become aggressive, directive can become dictatorial, and proactive can become reckless. To keep these tendencies in balance, high Dominance individuals can focus on being respectful when communicating and remember that maintaining key relationships is just as important as gaining results. They may also want to develop an action plan to restrain rash decisions.

Strengths—Those who have a high Dominance preference have significant strengths they can utilize during change. The Dominance style is proactive and ready to take on a challenge. They focus on results and are determined to make things happen. The Dominance style likes to win! Change can be approached as a challenge to be beat and an opportunity for victory. High Dominance individuals also radiate confidence. Confidence is a tremendous asset, especially during times of instability. Rising to the challenge, pursuing achievement, and moving ahead with confidence can create a new and better reality. These strengths are also powerful within an organizational team. Using the Dominance style effectively, an individual can challenge and lead an entire team toward achievement.

Influence

Challenges—High Influence individuals are expressive, flexible, adept at relating to others, and like freedom from details. They also are strongly motivated by praise. Consequently, they are concerned about maintaining a positive image and good relationships. During change, both image and relationships can be threatened. When the Influence style feels this danger, expressive and adept can become emotional and manipulative. Added to that, flexibility and lack of focus on details can slide into distractibility and disorganization. Those with an Influence preference can improve their success by pausing to reflect before reacting, concentrating on their positive value, and developing methods to stay focused.

Strengths—Those with an Influence style have valuable assets to offer during change. Foremost, they seek variety and are very flexible. Even more, they are optimistic and positive. The Influence style is not disturbed by rapidly changing events. Instead they can be excited by all the new possibilities. They are also excellent at developing new relationships, and they have a winsome charm. Change can be an exciting experience offering lots adventures, new connections, and new opportunities. These talents can foster personal and group success. High Influence individuals can use their positive outlook and motivational skills to inspire an entire team toward a new vision.

Steadiness

Challenges—Those with a Steadiness preference highly value stability and cooperation. They are accommodating, helpful, and loyal. Their approach is methodical and cautious; they do not make speedy decisions. Change brings instability, stirs up conflict, and requires adaptation. Those with a Steadiness preference may be disturbed by these disruptions. Their stability can become immobility, their cooperation can become submission, and their caution can become indecision. In addition, their loyalty can override their ability to make new alliances and adopt a new vision. High Steadiness individuals will adapt to change more productively if they focus on positives that will remain or can be carried into a new situation. They will also greatly benefit from learning to accept conflict and stand up for themselves. Lastly, they will advance their adjustment if they use their methodical approach to strategize timely responses and actions.

Strengths—Those with a Steadiness preference have enduring valuable qualities. First and foremost, they are stable and methodical. They will have loyalty to an organization when others may abandon ship. Additionally, they work well with others and are tremendous listeners. These skills help them gain the confidence of other people and be a great support to others during times of change. For their own benefit they can use these strengths to steadily build a new foundation, reinforce relationships, and regain the stability they enjoy. On a team, they can be a tremendous asset. High Steadiness individuals will support the needs of the team during change when many are focused solely on their own concerns. Their support and diplomacy provide a caring refuge in the midst of the change storm. Their perseverance and loyalty can foster the stability that both they and others need while events unfold.

Conscientiousness

Challenges—Highly Conscientious individuals are precise, cautious, and focused on quality. They want to do things right. During times of change, standards, tasks, and roles are in flux. It can be difficult to know what to do, how to do it, and how to do it well. Events can appear random and illogical. This can be especially frustrating in a work setting. Sometimes organizations launch initiatives, then radically change course or make a complete U-turn back to the old way of doing things. When the Conscientiousness style is faced with these disruptions, precision can become picky, cautious can become resistant, and a focus on quality can become an expectation of perfection. With their naturally careful approach, the Conscientiousness style is likely to see many danger signs during change. They can become negative, affecting both their mood and the mood of those around them. In their effort to maintain quality, they may become critical of themselves and others. Those who have a Conscientiousness preference can improve their success by relaxing their need to maintain order, learning to accept risks and becoming more forgiving of imperfect situations and people.

Strengths—The Conscientiousness style has excellent merits. When we are faced with change, doing it right is a big plus. The style's strong analytical skills are a great asset as well. When faced with challenging decisions during times of change, who better to evaluate and strategize the best course of action? Even more, the Conscientiousness style demonstrates great capacity to remain objective. It is the High Conscientiousness individual who is able to remain logical and strategic while others are reacting emotionally to the changes. The structure, quality, and logic of those with the Conscientiousness style enable them to plan and pursue high-quality achievement. Conscientiousness can be a tremendous benefit in an organizational team. During times of disruption, the ability to analyze and a focus on preserving quality are critical factors in maintaining competence and viability. When a team feels like they are navigating a ship through storm, an expert sailor is indispensable.

Working Together to Navigate Change

Navigating a ship is a great example of how all the styles can benefit each other and the team. The ship needs Dominance leaders and Influence motivators to take the lead and inspire the group to action with enthusiasm. The ship would not get very far nor would it be a pleasant trip without leaders and motivators. The ship also needs someone who will help the group cooperate and someone who will study the instruments and the navigation. The care of Steadiness and the precision of Conscientiousness keep the group working together and keep the ship from taking a wrong turn. Not only do the different styles benefit the team but also they benefit individuals in the team. When the Conscientiousness style wants to stay in the port and study the weather charts, waiting for perfect sailing day, the Dominance style can helpfully prod action. When the Influence style is impatient to jump into the dinghy to explore an uncharted island, the Steadiness style can diplomatically encourage a more measured and careful plan.

When we recognize the value of others' strengths and our need for balance, we are able to embrace the differences and view them as benefits rather than annoyances. The keys to individual and team success regarding personal style, especially during change, are awareness, appreciation, and respect. Individuals who view themselves as better or more right than others have a hard time admitting their own limitations and appreciating differences in others. Top performers are secure in their strengths and acknowledge their challenges. They also can much more easily embrace the strengths of others and benefit from the balance they can offer.

REFLECTION QUESTIONS

1. Which of the four DiSC styles do you think is your preferred style?
2. How does having this style impact you during times of change?
3. How might you adapt your style to deal with change?

Exercise

Sometimes it is difficult to see our own style. Find someone you trust who knows you well and let them read this chapter. Afterwards, ask them to tell you which of the four styles seem to describe you best. If you disagree with their assessment then ask several others to do the same. If they all think you are that style then they are probably right!

In addition, if you want to receive a personalized DiSC Classic profile, you can find instructions for doing so at our website: www.advantagecoaching.com.

CHAPTER 6

TAKING CHARGE

"Destiny is not a matter of chance. It is a matter of choice. It is not a thing to be waited for, it is a thing to be achieved."
—*William Jennings Bryan*

Top performers know that adapting to different surroundings and different people is key to becoming a change champion. However, it is equally important to take charge as a change champion.

During change, many things feel out of control. That sense of decreased control creates much of the frustration and anxiety that comes with change. Actually, we have much more control than we realize. In fact, we have 100 percent power over the three forces that drive our response to change—the power to *choose*, *believe*, and *act*. These forces interact and direct our ultimate psychological outcome as illustrated below:

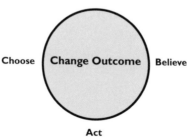

Choose, believe, and act move around the circle like a spinning Frisbee. Our beliefs will drive our choices and our actions. Likewise, our choices will direct our actions and impact our beliefs. Lastly, our actions will reinforce our beliefs and our choices.

A Frisbee not only spins, it also progresses. Fans of Frisbee Golf know if you spin the Frisbee well, it can sail a long distance, even landing with precision at an intended target. If you throw the Frisbee poorly, it will dive right to the ground. To be a change champion we need to engage our response to change with intention, purpose, and skill. Top performers will choose intentionally, believe strategically, and act productively, and the circle will spin upward toward the target of choice.

The Relationship between Choices and Values

We constantly make choices. Within the first minutes of waking we make many choices, like how long to stay in bed, what to wear, what to eat, and how to start the tasks for the day. Sometimes we get lost in the small choices and forget to evaluate the bigger choices that impact our life values and direction.

Occasionally we hold values or expectations that we have not examined closely. They have been quietly absorbed into our existence through early life lessons, personal experiences, or the larger culture.

An example of this is how different cultures interact in business. Recently, when I was performing workshops in South Korea, I was intrigued by the way they exchanged business cards. Here in the United States we grab the card, maybe write something on it, and then throw it in our pocket. In South Korea, they would never do this! They treat the business card with great respect. When you are handed the card you receive it with both hands (often adding a bow), study the card to make sure you are acknowledging their position, and then place the card gently in a place of prominence. In South Korea, the way they value position and authority are shown in the handling of a business card. Their values and expectations would cause them to see Americans' casual handling of business cards as an insult. Like cultural norms, each of us has a foundation of expectations that drives our behavior. If these remain unexamined, we may accidentally blunder in a more serious way than mishandling a business card.

Change is like entering a new culture. We enter the change carrying our expectations and values with us, often without much awareness. Lack of awareness risks two kinds of mistakes. The first is making a mistake by operating on automatic pilot. Americans on automatic pilot will offend their Korean counterparts by haphazardly tossing a business card in their pocket. During change our automatic-pilot assumptions may not be the most effective. Examining them will increase our adaptability and success. The second mistake is operating out of fear. As we discussed in chapter 3, change disturbs our fundamental security. During these periods it is easy to react by grasping for things that seem to offer relief. If our livelihood feels threatened we may focus on financial relief. During a job transition we may be tempted to jump at the first position that promises good financial reward, even if the job itself is unappealing. If our esteem or confidence is shaken we may look for power, recognition, or status. When companies are reorganized people often cling to an old title or position rather than moving toward a new growth opportunity. Unexamined expectations and values can lead to either unintentional or reactive mistakes. When we examine our values and goals we can use change as an opportunity to pursue long-term fulfillment and satisfaction.

Pursuing fulfillment is like building a house. Houses come in all shapes, sizes, and styles. Each builder can make a house to his own liking. However, we know that a quality house will have a solid foundation, sturdy walls, and a watertight roof. These building principles apply to all houses. Fulfillment also has principles. Edward Diener, a psychologist at the University of Illinois, has been studying satisfaction for two decades. He has found that appealing temptations are often not fulfilling. They are happiness distracters instead of happiness attractors. Chief happiness distracters are money and pleasure. Despite their universal allure, money and possessions do not bring fulfillment. Only extreme poverty diminishes happiness. Once basic needs are met there is little difference in satisfaction between the middle-class and the wealthy. Diener personally interviewed the members of the Forbes 400 (the four hundred wealthiest Americans) and found that despite their extreme wealth, they were not significantly happier than the general public. This connection is widespread. Census data shows that while material wealth has risen since World War II, the number of people who consider themselves happy is the same.

Americans have more money and more possessions but we are not happier because of them. If we exaggerate the value of wealth, we can be very vulnerable when our financial situation shifts.

Equally illusory is the pursuit of pleasure. As Seligman notes in his book on authentic happiness, pursuing personal pleasure has the least impact on long-term happiness. Much more important than pleasure are engagement (being invested in your relationships and activities) and meaning (using your talents for a larger purpose beyond personal gratification). Happiness distracters direct our energies toward acquisition: more money, more recognition, or more pleasure. During change we can over-focus on acquisition (income, security, esteem) and miss the long-term happiness that is achieved by pursuing larger goals.

Staying Grounded during Change

What does bring satisfaction? Like Seligman, Diener has found that long-term happiness is discovered when focusing beyond self. The foundations of happiness include:

- Good relationships
- Hope
- Meaning
- Spirituality

Seligman summarizes happiness as "the emotion that arises when we do something that stems from our strengths and virtues."

Rick Warren's story exemplifies how carefully chosen values can be a foundation for managing drastic change successfully. Warren had a rapid rise to fame and fortune. He is the founding pastor of Saddleback Church in California. His book *The Purpose Driven Life* was published in 2002 and quickly became a bestseller. By 2005, 26 million copies had sold and it was the best selling hardcover book of all time. *U.S.News & World Report* interviewed Rick in an October 2005 feature naming him as one of America's twenty-five best leaders. During the interview Rick relayed the effect of his success on his life. "It brought in a *ton* of money," said Rick. "The first thing we decided was that we wouldn't let it change our lifestyle one bit." He and his family remained in the same house. "Next, I stopped taking a salary from the church. Then I added up all the church had paid me in the previous twenty-five years and I gave it back." Taking it a step further, the Warrens started "reverse tithing." They give 90 percent of their income away, living on only 10 percent. The next challenge was how to handle instant fame. Rick turned to his faith and scripture for guidance. In a September 2005 interview with *Christianity Today*, he discusses what his examination uncovered saying, "I found those two thousand verses on the poor. How did I miss that? I went to a Bible college, two seminaries, and I got a doctorate. How did I miss God's compassion for the poor? I was not seeing all the purposes of God." Rick is now determined to use his newfound influence to battle the global scourges of spiritual emptiness, corruption, poverty, disease, and illiteracy.

When bombarded with change, Rick chose to focus on values beyond his personal security and pleasure. He chose to pursue purpose. Most of us do not encounter such dramatic windfalls, but we face the same kind of choices as Rick. Where is our security and satisfaction placed? When our world suddenly shifts, what we grab for and hold on to will determine our ultimate success and our satisfaction. There is a direct relationship between the values we pursue and the happiness that we achieve. Top performers ground themselves in satisfying values that lead to happiness and positive outcomes.

Up to this point we have discussed big picture motivations, warnings, perceptions, and ideals. We hope that you have been completing the reflection questions along the way. If you have, then you have been building a foundation for success. Now it is time to move to practicalities. For those who have been waiting to focus concretely on how to succeed, we have arrived! Our psychological outcome is determined by how we choose, how we believe, and how we act. Remember, we have 100 percent control of these forces. In the remaining pages and in the appendix you will have the opportunity to develop action steps toward becoming a top-performing change champion. Now let's start with how top performers choose, believe, and act.

Choose Intentionally

The first choice we make is how to respond to the change in our life. In chapter 2 we laid out the choice differences between change victims and change champions. Change champions intentionally choose to focus on what will bring them success and satisfaction.

These choices should be like the items we carry around in daily life. We are very intentional about what we carry with us. We pick briefcases and bags that will properly hold our supplies. We carry date books, cell phones, pens, watches, laptops, and all the things that will support our productive work. We would never carry around things that would keep us from being productive. Would you carry around a broken laptop or a slow watch or a pen without ink? Of course not!

This is so obvious it seems ridiculous to mention. Yet, we aren't always so practical when it comes to the choices that we carry every day. During times of change it is especially important that we fill our pockets with helpful choices and leave behind the choices that will drag us down. Imagine that you are in front of your bureau and you have to pick your choices to carry each morning. The good and bad are lying there together. Sometimes the bad ones are tempting because they are familiar and comfortable, like an old pair of sneakers. As much as we may love those worn sneakers, we don't wear them if we intend to win a race. Top performers understand that choices are tools and will choose the best available, even if it means discarding old favorites. In the next section we will learn how to make smart intentional choices. The first order of business is to choose your focus, activity, and path. These are the foundation on which you will build your success. Thankfully, we have good guidance on smart choices in these areas. Let's dive in!

Focus

• *Change champions choose Optimism over Pessimism*

Optimism not only feels good, it is good for you. Barbara Fredrickson, a psychologist at the University of Michigan, studies the impact of positive and negative emotions. Her experiments show that negative emotions generate narrow thinking and limit problem solving. Positive emotions broaden thinking and increase creative problem solving. The creative problem solving in turn reinforces positive feelings so that the two build on each other. The more positive we are, the more we are able to creatively problem solve. The more we problem solve, the more positive we feel.

Most people can't decide to feel positive or optimistic on a moment's notice. It doesn't work to give ourselves an order: "Just feel happy!" Feelings don't respond to orders, but feelings do respond to focus. Choose to focus on the positives. When we focus on the positives we open the door to optimism. This starts a process that produces hopeful emotions, creativity, and problem solving.

When changes occur, top performers know that by focusing on the opportunities in the change, they will positively impact themselves and their success.

Activity

- **Change champions choose Proaction over Reaction**

Change champions will also choose proaction over reaction. Success and satisfaction are closely linked with setting goals and working to achieve them. At the University of Missouri, Ken Sheldon's research has found that setting and achieving a progression of goals permanently boosts well-being. Even when failures occur, people are better able to return to and maintain happiness if they set goals and pursue them. This is most true when the goals reflect personal interests and values.

In addition, challenge and concentration invoke a positive mood dubbed "flow" by Mihaly Csikszentmihalyi, Director of Quality of Life Research Center in California. Flow can be found in any situation where people focus, engage, and concentrate. Unfortunately, many people fail to incorporate flow into their lives because they view passive activities (like watching TV) as more appealing, even though these don't bring long-term satisfaction. Choosing proaction is win-win! Not only does setting goals and concentrating on achieving them promote success, it makes us feel good too. Average performers take a wait-and-see attitude. Top performers are proactive. They set goals and concentrate on achieving them.

Path

- **Change champions choose Fulfillment over Fear**

As we discussed in chapter 3 and earlier in this chapter, powerful fears can arise during change. Fearing the loss of money, job, status, comfort, reputation,

[71]

and relationships tempts us to follow the path of fear. If we believe that our personal value, satisfaction, and security come from possessions (standard of living), position (job or title), or power (control), we can be seriously shaken when change threatens the status quo. This is the moment when choice is critical. We can choose to succumb to irrational fear and chase illusions, or we can choose to pursue fulfillment. All the research shows that possessions, position, and power do not bring long-lasting satisfaction. Long-term fulfillment is gained through building good relationships, developing meaning, and living with purpose. Top performers will use choice and reason to overcome irrational fears and tempting illusions. They will choose to pursue fulfillment and live with purpose.

The first step to becoming a top-performing change champion is to choose and choose intentionally. Not all choices are equal. In the appendix you will have an opportunity to work more concretely on your choices for focus, activity, and path. In the meantime, take a moment to reflect on your values. What are your driving values? Are they satisfying you in the long term? Do you find yourself pursuing things that seem appealing, but ultimately are not fulfilling? If so, you might reflect on things that engage you, provide purpose, and are meaningful. When you are ready, move on to the next step: believing strategically.

Believe Strategically

Beliefs are just as important as choices. In fact, they are closely linked. When we choose optimism, we decide to look for positives and choose to believe that the future has bright possibilities. Beliefs and choices are so closely linked it can be hard to tell which comes first. Do beliefs drive choices or do choices compel beliefs? The answer is both! Our choices do impact our beliefs and our beliefs will drive our choices. A change champion will make choices and adopt beliefs that work together to promote success, just like a good diet and exercise work together to bring fitness and health.

What beliefs promote success during times of change? Like people who are lucky and happy, people who have faced challenges have been studied. Some people succumb. Others rise above difficulties and adapt remarkably well despite adversity. Those who succeed are called thrivers. Thrivers show a common pattern of beliefs and expectations that enable them to excel through challenge. These attitudes create a powerful mix of resilience during times of challenge and support the six disciplines of top performers: grieve, forgive, accept, plan, act, and build. Paul Pearsall, a neuropsychologist describes the four operating beliefs of thrivers:

I. Let It Go

Thrivers experience just as much pain, anxiety, and depression as everyone else. They are not immune to bad feelings. The difference is they do not let bad feelings become quicksand that draws them deeper and deeper into a pit. Rather than avoiding the feelings, they avoid getting stuck in the feelings. The ability of thrivers to let it go supports two critical practices of top performers: grieve and forgive. When we grieve we are allowing ourselves to feel the pain and work through it. When we forgive we are preventing ourselves from becoming victims of the pain. Forgiveness allows us to let it go and move on.

2. Have Faith

One of the reasons thrivers are able to let it go is they seem to understand the bad feelings will not last forever. Having faith supports and builds on the choice to choose optimism over pessimism. We can choose optimism because we believe that better days are to come. From chapter 3 we know that believing that our difficulties are permanent kills adaptation. Thrivers have faith that brighter days will come.

3. Accommodate

Thrivers understand that a good reality does not have to be the same reality. The ability to accommodate includes two additional top-performer disciplines: accept and plan. When we accommodate we accept that change brings a new "normal." Change champions and thrivers adjust their expectations and plan accordingly. Instead of getting frustrated and bitter from constantly trying to regain what is past, they realign their expectations and get pleasure from the new present.

4. Gain in Pain

"No pain, no gain" is the motto of thrivers. The final two disciplines of act and build are supported by the belief of "gain in pain." Thrivers and top performers understand that challenges and adversity bring strength that is to be valued. They view challenges as an opportunity for growth rather than a threat. They believe that they can overcome the challenges and will be stronger as a result, even while experiencing great pain. Pearsall uses a quote by Beethoven to exemplify this idea: "I can defy this fate even though there will be times when I shall be the unhappiest of God's creatures." Top performers accept that the path to success requires tenacity and value the growth they achieve by pushing through the challenge.

Thrivers are not special people with extraordinary skills. In fact, many thrivers came from circumstances with few resources and little support. They thrived because they held the four "thriving" beliefs and acted out of those beliefs. Can thriving be learned? Yes! We can choose to build beliefs that will support thriving.

There are several techniques that support thriving beliefs:

1. Focus on what you can control

Resilient people are aware they cannot control life, but they can control themselves. They focus on what they are able to control and work to contribute to their own success. If you want to be a top performer during change you will focus on what you can control.

2. Gather gratitude

A large part of having faith is appreciating the positives in life. We won't get stuck in pessimism if we dwell on what we appreciate. There is a lot of wisdom in Johnson Oatman's 1897 children's song "Count Your Blessings," with the familiar refrain, "Count your blessings, name them one by one." Psychologist Robert Emmons studied gratitude at the University of California. He found that people who regularly wrote down as few as five things that they were grateful for were less stressed, healthier, more joyful, and more optimistic. The "let it go" and "have faith" beliefs are built from the discipline of gathering gratitude. When we are grateful we are less resentful of the past and more positive about the future. Change champions will take time to gather gratitude.

3. Focus on strengths

Steven and Sybil Wolin, codirectors of Project Resilience, have found that acknowledging and focusing on strengths is critical to thriving. Sadly, most people are not aware of their strengths. According to Ken Tucker of the Gallup Organization, 80 percent of people are not able to identify their own strengths. Fortunately, those in the resilience field have developed a framework for identifying strengths. Edith Grothberg, who heads an international resilience project, suggests thinking in three categories: *I have* (not just possessions but relationships, mentors, and all resources), *I am* (qualities, values, gifts), and *I can* (all talents and skills including relational and emotional).

Believing strategically will promote smart choices and lead to productive actions. To be a top performer during change you will build the four thriving beliefs by focusing on areas you can control, gathering gratitude, and using your strengths.

The story of Sergeant Alvin York, a soldier during WWI, highlights the power of using our strengths. York and only fifteen other men were charged with taking out enemy machine-gun placements during the war. As they advanced, half of the men were taken down by enemy fire, including the troop leader. York had a unique strength; he was an expert marksman. Ignoring the machine-gun bullets whizzing by, he stood, aimed, and fired each time an enemy gunner appeared. He and the few remaining troops disabled 35 machine gun units and captured 132 enemy soldiers. York faced overwhelming odds in a dangerous situation without many resources. Rather than giving up, he utilized the strengths he had to strategically solve the problem and produced victory for himself and his comrades.

Act Productively

Wise choices and strategic beliefs provide the energy and goals for action. When getting ready for a trip, you need to set your destination (goal) and fill up on gas (gather energy). You also need directions on how to get there—a tactical plan so to speak. Productive action is your tactical plan. Productive action can be summed up in four words: Ready, Realize, Review, Recruit.

Ready

Change creates a new reality. Before action can be effective it is important to pause to assess the situation and gather resources. We need to ask ourselves some basic questions:

- "What do I need?"
- "What resources do I already have?"
- "Where can I get additional resources?
- "What do I want?"

Referring back to the behavioral styles discussed in chapter 5, those who prefer a Steadiness or Conscientiousness style might have an easier time with the preparation phase and have a challenge moving on. Those who have a Dominance or Influence preference may find this important phase tiresome and be tempted to skip directly to action. Whatever your preference, good assessment will help you better determine and achieve goals.

Realize

Once we have surveyed the landscape, we need to set goals for moving toward the destination. Goal-setting provides energy, purpose, and satisfaction. It also is essential to getting us where we want to go. Good goal-setting includes short- and long-term goals that are SMART:

- Specific
- Measurable
- Achievable
- Relevant
- Timed

Specific goals are concrete and precise and help fulfill a larger purpose. "I want to succeed during this organizational transition" is a good purpose but a vague goal. A more specific goal might be "I want to improve my career path by using this transition to gain a promotion to executive director by the end of the year." *Measurable* means everyone can know what has been achieved. "Within two weeks I want to volunteer to lead a cross-functional team" is measurable. *Achievable* goals are those that are realistic. "I want to talk about the possibility of a promotion with my boss this month" is achievable. "I want to be promoted this week" is probably not. *Relevant* goals are those that provide significant progress toward the larger goals. Relevant goals help prioritize our time wisely. For example, if a job layoff becomes a possibility, staying gainfully employed is a larger goal. Two related relevant goals would be to update your resume and refresh your network of contacts. A less relevant goal is to focus only on daily tasks within the current job. Finally, *timed* goals provide accountability. It is critical that goals be timed so that we provide ourselves with the incentive to keep moving forward.

Review

Review is part of the process that top performers do automatically. A great deal of dissatisfaction, frustration, and pessimism develops when we do not adjust to the ever-changing realities we face. Thrivers are able to hold a "positive realism." This positive realism maintains optimism but adjusts expectations to current realities. Review is an ongoing process that assesses and adapts based on new realities. Review can happen at any point when events block or divert our intended goals. For example, if you were expecting a promotion shortly only to discover that your company is preparing for a significant downsizing, a review is in order.

Review is not a pessimistic acceptance of defeat. It is a realignment of your expectations and actions based on new information. We all experience setbacks, but setbacks do not have to stall progress. Top performers know that change champions absorb setbacks and adjust their course to create opportunities based on new facts.

Recruit

As mentioned earlier, thrivers have commonalities that determine their success. The single biggest plus for thrivers is support and community. Not one thriver achieves alone. All thrivers recruited help from others around them. Supporters provided the thrivers with empathy, aid, accountability, objectivity, perspective, and encouragement. Top performers purposefully gather support that will encourage and promote their success.

I worked with one top performer named Sean who was managing a major business unit for a Fortune 500 company. He was informed one day that most of his competitors were getting out of similar businesses and that his parent company had decided to do the same. A lesser performer might have panicked and become helpless. Sean did the opposite. He saw this as a time to show his worth to the organization and capture his competitors' losses.

Sean spent time in the *Ready* phase analyzing trends, business challenges, and potential profits and losses. In the *Realize* mode, he set the goal of talking the parent company out of closing down the business by showing them the gap left in the market by their competitors. Through the many meetings, obstacles, and naysayers, he *Reviewed* the current realities and absorbed the setbacks and resistance. He made major cutbacks in his department and knew that he had to let some people go. Being a top performer, he did not try to handle this business transition alone. Sean *Recruited* partners and advocates to help him make his case.

After years of battle, Sean got the result he had envisioned. He was able to take a hopeless situation and turn it around. He now runs one of the most profitable businesses within this Fortune 500 company. The business is very different then it was years ago and he has been through an incredible amount of change, but Sean weathered the storm, saved many people's jobs, and turned a losing business into one that is respected by his clients and continues to grow. Top performers know how to ready, realize, review, and recruit.

We have covered a lot of ground in this chapter. We encourage you to ponder all the facets of choose, believe, and act. It may be helpful to go back over the chapter and focus on one area at a time. It is likely that you will need to implement the ideas incrementally using SMART goals. Feel free to give yourself time to develop skills in one area before tackling another. The following reflection questions and the appendix will help you work out the specifics to develop an action plan. You may want to add to our suggestions by creating additional actions steps. The tools are in your hands. Top performers become change champions by using their 100 percent power to direct their outcome. We are confident that if you discipline yourself to choose intentionally, believe strategically, and act productively, you will be a top-performing change champion.

REFLECTION QUESTIONS

Let's focus first on the three techniques we covered that can help you build a thriving mindset during times of change: focusing on what you can control, showing gratitude, and realizing your strengths.

1. Thinking of your current situation, make a list of three to five things that you can impact or control that will help you do well in the situation.

2. Find a quiet spot and meditate in silence. Repeat the phrase, "I am grateful for _____" (filling in the blank with something new each time). After you are done, write down the things for which you are grateful here:

I am grateful for _____

I am grateful for _____

I am grateful for _____

I am grateful for _____

List others if applicable:

3. Make a list of your top strengths.

a. I have _____, _____, and _____.

b. I am _____, _____, and _____.

c. I can _____, _____, and _____.

Now, how can you use these strengths to help cope with the change you are going through and even find opportunity during this time?

CHAPTER 7

IMPACTING OTHERS IN TIMES OF CHANGE

"The community stagnates without the impulse of the individual. The impulse dies away without the sympathy of the community."
—William James

Up until now we have focused on the impact of change for the individual. In this chapter, we want to look beyond ourselves to the bigger picture of organizational change. An organization can be a family, a community group, or a work place. Individual change and organizational change are tightly connected. All individual changes multiply to impact an organization, and organizational change ripples out to effect individuals.

Doing the Wave

An analogy to this is the wave. When we go to big sporting events we commonly see the wave appear in the stadium. The wave is a living group experience. Some time during the event, a small group of people in the stands will rise up, sweeping their arms in the air. On cue, the next group of fans will follow and the next and the next. It starts out small, but as people catch on, the wave grows to include the entire stadium full of spectators. From a distance the whole stadium appears to be rising and falling in a giant wave of people.

Waves are awesome forces. They can be both majestic and fierce. If you have ever been at the ocean around the time of a storm, you know the power and breathtaking splendor of tremendous waves. Surfers travel the world to harness the incredible power of the wave and achieve unbelievable feats on a surfboard. We also know the destructive power of waves. If waves overpower their natural boundaries, they can wreak havoc on surrounding communities.

Organizational change has the same potential for achievement or destruction. Change that is not harnessed positively can create a flood within a group. Change that is led and channeled can be a dynamic power that lifts the entire group to high achievement. The stadium wave works because someone starts and leads the spectators to follow. Change in organizations happens much the same way. Change champions have the power to create success for themselves and lead an entire wave of success within their group. Top performers can be more than champions, they can also be change leaders.

Champions and Leaders

There is a difference between a champion and a leader. A champion achieves personal success. He or she wins a personal race or personal trophy, real or symbolic. We have athletic, business, social, and political champions. Everyone recognizes them as winners. Classic champions are Venus and Serena Williams in tennis, Bill Gates in business, Sean Connery in acting, and John F. Kennedy in politics. Leaders are more than champions. Leaders create good for many, not just themselves.

Are there many leaders in times of change? Sadly, change leaders are in the minority. Most are change deserters. During organizational change most people (up to 80 percent) actively or passively resist change. The majority act like donkeys or rabbits. When a donkey decides it has had enough, it digs in its heels and uses all its force to resist moving forward. Donkeys will spend an enormous amount of energy working to stand still. Rabbits, on the other hand, will use all their energy to run and hide. If you have ever seen a rabbit chased by a dog you know that they can sprint at an unbelievable pace and scurry into the smallest places to avoid capture. Unfortunately, most people use their energy to resist or run. Only about 10 to 20 percent are top performers who will move to the front to support and promote change.

At this point you may be thinking, "So what? If I want to resist or run, what is wrong with that?" Resisting or running may seem like the personally safe thing to do, but it can actually be self-defeating. Organizational change is like an avalanche. In an avalanche, the correct life-saving response is not what most people think. Our first instinct would be to dive and hide or brace and resist. Both these responses are dangerous. If you dive and hide you are likely to get buried alive. If you brace and resist you are likely to get crushed. Unbelievably, the life-saving response is to leap into the avalanche and actually swim with it like you are swimming in water. To survive, you join the avalanche by leaping in and working with the forces. During the avalanche of organizational change we can become both change champions and change heroes by leaping in and leading the charge for others and ourselves.

All the skills we develop as change champions provide us with the foundation we need to be a change leader or hero. We liken a change hero to the image of a great warrior king. Great warrior kings have the foundation of personal battle skills so they are champions. Great warrior kings also have added skills that enable them to lead an entire league toward victory. Change leaders will take advantage of their battle skills, pick their battles, control the field, and rally the troops.

Battle Skills

Management research shows that change leaders are positive, open, relationally skilled, conscientious, and adaptable. They have strong emotional intelligence.

The idea of emotional intelligence was pioneered by psychologists Peter Salovey and John Mayer as a special set of emotional and relational skills beyond traditional intelligence. Daniel Goleman popularized the concept in his 1995 book *Emotional Intelligence*. Goleman describes emotional intelligence as "the capacity for recognizing our own feelings and those of others, for motivating ourselves, and for managing emotions well in ourselves and in our relationships." Emotional intelligence is a learned battle skill.

Business researchers have called for organizations to help employees develop specific skills that promote change leaders, like communication, confidence, conflict leadership, listening, and coaching skills. Some are hesitant to hire assistance to develop these skills in their leaders and staff. That's unfortunate, as 80 percent of all staff defections are caused by poor relationships with managers.

In addition, organizational studies have shown that top performers shine because of their superior soft skills. We define soft skills as nontechnical personal and relational skills. The ability to communicate effectively, manage time, resolve conflict, achieve goals, motivate a team, and lead people are all soft skills. A study of two hundred companies found that soft skills accounted for two-thirds of an employee's competence, while only one-third of the competence involved technical skill. In other words, exceptional relational skills were far more important than good technical skills. These skills impact the bottom line. One study of a multinational consulting firm found that those with above-average human-relations skills delivered $1.2 million more in company profits. So-called soft skills have a hard impact!

This is why we are so dedicated as professionals to helping individuals become top performers and leaders. These skills matter, and top performers know that training and coaching in soft skills impact their lives and the lives of those they lead. Change leaders hone their battle skills and provide opportunities for others to develop these critical skills.

Pick Your Battles

A good warrior does not waste energy and resources on losing campaigns. Change champions and change leaders show the same wisdom. In all situations personal, relational, and organizational, we have three interactions with control. There are things we can control, things we can influence, and things we can't control. Skilled change champions and leaders will understand the difference and respond effectively.

Misguided attempts at control cause many individual and organizational problems. These difficulties arise when people try to control what they can't, or don't step forward to control what they can. You may have had the experience of a supervisor who did not intervene to stop the harmful impact of another employee's problem behavior. Sometimes this is minor nagging concern, like an individual who is regularly a few minutes late. Other times it is a more serious case of poor performance or even neglect. The motivation, morale, and productivity of an entire team is affected by the lack of leadership in addressing such problems. Equally disturbing can be team members who try to exert control beyond their scope of responsibility. They do this by spreading rumors about others, tattling to a supervisor, or withholding information in an attempt to gain power through hoarding knowledge.

The balance of knowing when to pursue control and knowing when to release control is a difficult but critical skill. The following chart, adapted from Patti Hathaway's article "When You're at the End of Your Rope, Let Go!" displays the impact of pursuing and releasing control under different circumstances:

	Can't Control	Can Influence	Can Control
Pursue	Resent	Promote	Results
Release	Relief	Diminish	Retreat

1. Pursue

If we pursue things we can't control, we end up resentful. Even more, we can be a detriment to the entire team by misdirecting our efforts. If we pursue things we can influence, then we promote and support the organization and our success. Every team needs promoters and supporters. No leader can make it entirely alone. The most fabulous coach in the world cannot lead a team to victory if no one is willing to follow the coach's lead. Team members may have limited opportunities to control the *entire* team, but will have many opportunities to exert influence. Using influence correctly can have a powerful impact on team success. Finally, if we pursue the things we can control, our energy is correctly directed and will bring results. Top performers know this and use their considerable influence and actions to promote the organization and bring results.

2. Release
To release is the opposite of pursue. Sometimes we let it go when we have the opportunity to influence or control. If we release when we can influence, we may diminish the results of others. Influencers are like spectators at a game. The spectators create an energy that affects the entire team. Athletes know it is more challenging to play at the opposing team's arena. Every team gains strength, confidence, and success from the energetic support of the home-field spectators. Influencers, like spectators, can cheer the team to victory or jeer the team to defeat. We can also release when we have direct control. Releasing at that moment is a full-scale retreat, which will certainly guarantee defeat. However, there are key times when releasing is the perfect solution. Much energy is wasted and frustration felt when we exert control over areas that are beyond our direction. When we are wise enough to release control from areas that we cannot impact, we gain immediate relief. Energy can then be used to support and direct success.

Control the Field
A change champion controls his or her personal field by strategizing resources and using energy productively. A leader controls the organizational field by carefully utilizing the resources of the team. Military experts know that victory is achieved with well-skilled troops and good control of resources. Exhausted or poorly supplied

troops cannot succeed no matter how well trained. Organizational change is like a campaign; wasted resources and excessive shifting of strategies creates chaos.

Eric Abrahamson from Columbia University Business School has studied organizational change extensively. He has coined the phrase "repetitive change syndrome" to describe the problem of the poorly controlled change field. He uses the example of Jennifer, a midlevel telecom executive. Jennifer worked at AOL Time Warner. During a three-year period, the company had three CEOs. Each CEO launched different visions, initiatives, and plans. Jennifer's immediate manager changed four times. Teams of people swung in and out of favor as leadership changed. Plans and execution strategies were in constant flux. Even basic structures and processes were in constant motion. During this period there was only one stable truth: everything would change again in six months.

Clearly, productivity can be challenging under such circumstances. Mismanaging the field causes overload, chaos, and burnout. Abrahamson suggests that if employees are spending 30 percent or more of their time on change initiatives, then the change field is out of control. Change leaders will carefully monitor the amount of time they and their team are spending coping with change.

Rally the Troops

Change leaders and heroes do not achieve alone. Great warrior kings know that rallying the troops is essential to success. There are seven practices that will promote motivation and team engagement:

1. Project optimism

Change researchers have found that 80 percent of employees who felt good about a change acquired their positive attitude from their direct supervisor's positive influence. Everyone matters during change. Those who project optimism will influence their immediate coworkers and encourage optimism for the whole group.

2. Plan for people

Unfortunately, most change planning usually involves transition strategies for everything *except* the people affected. It is assumed that the people do not need to know much about the change in advance and that they will automatically engage when change is announced. Change leaders will make people's engagement and transition part of the planning process.

3. Speak to the personal

Organizational change impacts individuals first. No company truly exists if the building is standing empty. People need to connect personal gain or opportunity to the change. In fact, 69 percent of employees admit that they are always looking for better employment opportunities. The change hero will go beyond the organizational benefits and provide a picture of the personal opportunities that change can bring.

4. Take a pulse

Change research has found that most organizations do not take any measure of employee engagement. No one knows if the troops are fighting the battle or have left the field. There is no victory if the troops have deserted. A change hero will make a point of taking the pulse of the team.

5. Be a guide
Change opens up a new landscape. Direction and plans are unclear in uncharted territory. A change leader will provide guidance and information about new roles, task, expectations, and challenges.

6. Get and give support
Change success requires adaptability and new skills. Leaders and teams need support to adjust and develop needed skills. There are many consultants, trainers, and coaches available to support your efforts and build your performance.

7. Celebrate success
Organizational change causes extra stress, added burden, and increased challenges. People, processes, and systems are stretched, often without rest or encouragement. A change leader will take every opportunity to encourage by celebrating each success. The feeling of accomplishment is a powerful motivator and important reminder of the end goal and a view of victory.

Leading with Authority but No Title
We often think of change leaders as those with official titles and established authority. In fact, we sometimes leave all the change work to those who are in charge. But change heroes can arise from those with little apparent power.

Eleanor Roosevelt was a change hero. Roosevelt was born in 1884 at a time when women of her class were expected to be decorative cheerleaders for their husbands and mothers to their children. Her mother was a beautiful socialite who was embarrassed by her plain daughter and even gave her humiliating nicknames like Granny. Her father was an alcoholic. She was orphaned at ten and sent to boarding school in Europe. She returned to the United States as a young woman and married her cousin Franklin Delano Roosevelt in 1905.

Her husband became a prominent politician and entered the White House as president in 1933. Roosevelt was relegated to household duties and spent many years bearing and rearing their children. She had little official influence. In fact, she had little marital influence, as her husband had an extramarital relationship with her social secretary.

Yet despite holding no political office and living at a time when women were not welcomed in the world of men's affairs, Roosevelt used her influence to make profound changes. She believed in equal rights long before the civil rights movement. In 1943, she influenced the military to stop the segregation of all military recreational facilities. This began the systematic desegregation of the entire military, which led the nation in creating equal opportunity for all races. Roosevelt, a "mere woman" changed the face of the United States military.

What Makes a Top Performer?

When we think of a top performer we often think of a person who has experienced individual achievement or success. In truth, top performers impact those around them. They inspire others to greatness and they challenge others to accountability. Top performers know the value of their community and their impact upon that community.

In this book we have looked at how change is inevitable and is accelerating. We examined the choices that you can make in change and the dangers that can come from bad choices. We looked at how top performers increase their luck and opportunities during the twists and turns of this world. Finally, we walked through the attitudes, skills, and techniques that top performers use to thrive while others hide. These are the things that top performers know about change. And now you know them too! Whether you are already a top performer or are climbing the ladder to be one, we encourage you to remember the value of focusing on what you can control and confidently believing that you can impact your life and your future. You'll never regret this type of mindset and focus!

REFLECTION QUESTIONS

Top performers take account of their behaviors in order to grow to the next level. They welcome the chance to have their performance evaluated in order to see a vision for growth and success. Use the following questions to focus on yourself as a leader. Grade yourself on the following scales about the seven practices that motivate others.

A = Exceptional
B = Good
C = Average
D = Poor
F = Failing

Using these grades, how well are you:
Projecting optimism to others
Grade: _____

Planning for the people
Grade: _____

Speaking to the personal by providing a vision for personal opportunities during change
Grade: _____

Taking the pulse of the team
Grade: _____

Providing guidance and information for others
Grade: _____

Getting and giving support in the form of outside aides to your people
Grade: _____

Celebrating successes during the change
Grade: _____

As you rate yourself in these areas, how would you like to improve?

APPENDIX

CREATING YOUR PERSONAL APPROACH TO CHANGE

In this appendix we bring together the most important elements in each chapter to help you create a plan for dealing with change. We have written this appendix to mirror the chapters in the book so that you can return to that chapter if you need clarification or more information.

Chapter 1: Why Top Performers *Must* Know How to Deal with Change

1. Are you more of a homesteader or pioneer? Identify the strengths and challenges of your preference between these two.

Strengths	Challenges

2. How might you use the strengths of your preference to aid you in approaching change?
3. How can you compensate for your challenges (i.e., how can you gather support and resources to deal with change)?
4. In chapter 1 we described the following negative and positive outcomes to going through change. How do these apply to the change you are currently going through?

Negative Outcomes	Positive Outcomes
• Depression	• Enthusiasm
• Anxiety	• Hope
• Withdrawal	• Advancement
• Stagnation	• Growth
• Failure	• Transformation

Table 1.1: Negative and Positive Change Outcomes

Chapter 2: Change Choices

1. In chapter 2 we talked about six negative reactions to change. Which are your most prominent negative reactions? Rank the following list from one to six with 1 representing the negative reaction with which you struggle with the most and 6 the reaction that is the least problematic for you.

_____ Worry

_____ Deny

_____ Resist

_____ Retreat

_____ Blame

_____ Break

Extra credit: Find a few trusted friends, colleagues, or loved ones. Ask them if they agree with your ranked list or if they see you handling change differently. Discuss strategies with them for changing your negative reactions.

2. We also talked about various negative and positive perceptions about change. The following worksheet will walk you through your own perceptions of change. Simply think of change in general and

answer the questions. Make sure you do not leave any of the questions in the positive column blank.

Negative Perceptions	Positive Perceptions
In what way does change threaten you?	How might change enhance your life?
In what way does change confuse you?	How might you be excited about change?
In what way does change hurt you?	How might change strengthen you?
In what way does change take away from you?	How might change give to you?
In what way can change defeat you?	How might change create success for you?

Chapter 3: Change Dangers

1. Take a current change that you are going through and rank it on the following scales. In order to gain insight into the difference between feelings and reality, first circle the number that represents how you feel, but then also circle the number that represents what is really true (when you examine it more objectively). Be completely truthful and do not exaggerate.

In terms of the duration of the negative impact of this change, it will last…

1	2	3	4	5
Insignificantly	Briefly	Temporarily	For some time	Forever

In terms of what I can do about this change, I can impact…

1	2	3	4	5
Everything	Most things	Some things	Not much	Nothing

In terms of me being completely responsible for the change,

it is...

1	2	3	4	5
Not my fault	Somewhat my fault	Unsure	Mainly my fault	Completely my fault

In terms of impacting other areas of my life this event...

1	2	3	4	5
Is completely isolated	Has some impact	Has moderate impact	Has significant impact	Impacts all

Chapter 4: Increasing Your Luck during Times of Change

In chapter 4 we presented benefits to dealing well with change. Walk through the following worksheet to fully spell out those benefits for yourself.

Present Benefits

How will dealing well with this change help you succeed now?

How will dealing well with this change help you feel better?

How will dealing well with this change help you gain confidence?

How will dealing well with this change help you add skills?

How will dealing well with this change help you create opportunity?

How will dealing well with this change help you increase your strength?

Future Benefits

In the long term, how will dealing well with this change help you
move on to bigger successes?

In the long term, how will dealing well with this change help you
have less distress and an easier life?

In the long term, how will dealing well with this change help you
continue to build your confidence?

In the long term, how will dealing well with this change help you
become more adept in general?

In the long term, how will dealing well with this change help you
increase your openness to future opportunities?

In the long term, how will dealing well with this change help you
become more resilient?

Chapter 5: Adapting to Change

1. In this chapter we asked you to identify the strengths and challenges of your style. Look at the list of strengths of each of the styles. How might you adapt yourself to show a style different from your natural one to cope with change? To find out, do the following:

- Circle the strengths of one or two of the styles that you would like to show more of during times of change:

Dominance	• Proactive
	• Decisive
	• Likes challenge
	• Independent

Influence	• Likes variety
	• Inspiring
	• Flexible
	• Positive
Steadiness	• Steady
	• Diplomatic
	• Accommodating
	• Cautious
Conscientiousness	• Analytical
	• Cautious
	• Objective
	• Precise

• How can you use this ability during times of change?

• How will you go about building this strength? What resources are available to you for growing in this area? What training might you take to increase this skill?

Now take this list to a manager, colleague, or loved one and ask them for accountability to follow through with this plan.

2. Name three specific ways that you would like to adapt your natural style to better deal with change.

Chapter 6: Taking Charge

1. In this chapter we talked about the importance of your choices in the three areas of focus, activity, and path. Your choices were:

- Optimism vs. Pessimism
- Proaction vs. Reaction
- Fulfillment vs. Fear

Use the following chart to walk yourself through your choices related to a current change going on in your life:

Negative Choices
If I choose a pessimistic focus then I would view this change as...
If I choose reactive activity then I will...
If I want to walk down a path of fear then I will...

Positive Choices
If I choose an optimistic focus then I will see this change as...
If I choose to be proactive then I will...
If I want a path of fulfillment I will...

Use all of the statements in the positive column as positive mantras to help you through your change experience. Repeat them to yourself frequently and with feeling.

2. Review your exercises from this chapter, focusing on what you can control, what you are grateful for, and your strengths. Remember to apply these to any new change challenge.

3. Walk through the four R's to form a plan to deal with your current change.
- *Ready:* List what you need to move forward.
- *Realize:* Identify five to seven SMART goals for a set time frame (daily, weekly, or monthly).
- *Review:* What adjustments need to be made?
- *Recruit:* Who can support your success? List them here and contact them soon!

Chapter 7: Impacting Others in Times of Change

1. In our final chapter we looked at you as a change agent in your organization or other setting. One important skill set was emotional intelligence. Rate yourself on the following soft skills. Circle a 7 if you are superior at the skill. Circle a 1 if you are horrible. Circle other numbers if you are like most of us and somewhere between these two.

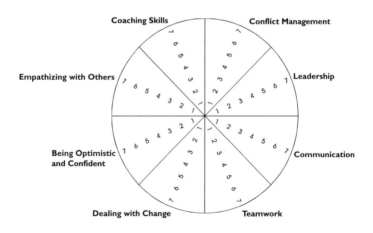

Now connect the dots on your wheel. If this were a tire of your car, how well would it drive? What kind of mentoring, reading, training, or coaching could you pursue to grow in these skills?

2. In this chapter we also talked about rallying the troops by projecting optimism, planning for the people, speaking to the personal, taking a pulse, being a guide, getting and giving support, and celebrating success. Walk through each of these seven methods to build your insight and take your behaviors to the next level.

- Give three examples of how you are projecting optimism to others in the current change situation.
- How are you planning for the people or influencing leadership of the need to plan for the people?
- Give a detailed example of how you are working to provide a picture of the personal opportunities that change can bring to people.
- Top performers also take a pulse to see how the troops are doing. Write down the names of three people who you want to pursue to see how they are doing.
- What are some additional behaviors that you could be showing right now that would brand you as a guide who is helping others through the change? Try to name at least three.
- How are you pursuing support or influencing leadership to pursue support to help others work through the change experience (consultants, books, trainers, coaches, mentors, etc.)?
- Name three additional ways that you could lead others by celebrating successes despite the stress of change.

If you have completed your change management plan, congratulations. We wish you the best in your journey to become a top performer during times of change!

ABOUT THE AUTHORS

Tim Ursiny, PhD, CBC, RCC

Tim Ursiny is the CEO of Advantage Coaching & Training. He is a coach/trainer specializing in helping people reach peak performance, great relationships, and personal happiness. Dr. Tim regularly speaks for Fortune 500 companies wanting workshops that are practical yet entertaining. He also coaches CEOs, executives, sales professionals, and others on a variety of subjects related to performance and life satisfaction. Dr. Tim's previous books include *The Confidence Plan: How to Build a Stronger You, The Coach's Handbook,* and *The Coward's Guide to Conflict,* which is currently in its third printing and has been translated into several foreign languages. He is currently writing a series of books called *What Top Performers Know about... .* This is the first of that series. Other topics include conflict and public speaking skills. He lives in Wheaton, Illinois, with his wife, Marla, and his three sons, Zach, Colton, and Vance. Dr. Tim can be reached at Drtim@advantagecoaching.com.

Barbara A. Kay, MA, LPC, RCC

Barbara Kay is an executive coach and trainer with Advantage Coaching & Training. She combines her business and professional psychology background to bring excellence, achievement, growth, and fulfillment to individuals and organizations. Barbara coaches individuals, entrepreneurs, and executives to develop their talents and energize their success. In her work with large and small organizations, Barbara trains teams in a wide variety of areas including communication, coaching, conflict, and change. Her goal is to develop dynamic, fun, and powerful teams. She has published articles in professional publications and speaks for corporate groups and professional associations. *The Top Performer's Guide to Change* is Barbara's first book. In her free time, Barbara volunteers in her church and enjoys family time with her husband, Bob, and sons, Tom, William, and Charles.

Advantage Coaching & Training provides workshops, team facilitation, and personal coaching to help individuals and organizations deal with change and excel at communication. You can reach Tim and Barbara at:

Advantage Coaching & Training
490 East Roosevelt Road Suite 102
West Chicago, IL 60186
www.advantagecoaching.com
800-657-5904

BIBLIOGRAPHY

Abrahamson, Eric. "Avoiding Repetitive Change Syndrome," *MIT Sloan Management Review* 45, no. 2, 93–5 (Winter 2004).

Atkinson, Philip. "Managing resistance to change," *Management Services* 49, no. 1 (Spring 2005).

Baker, Dan PhD and Stauth Cameron. *What Happy People Know.* Rodale, Inc. 2003.

Blum, Deborah. "Finding Strength: How to Overcome Anything," *Psychology Today* (May/June 1998): 32+.

Borysenko, Joan. "Rethinking Change," *Prevention* (Emmaus, Pa.) 56, no. 7 97–9 (Jl 2004): 97–9.

Bryant, Melanie and Julie Wolfram Cox. "Conversion Stories as Shifting Narratives of Organizational Change," *Journal of Organizational Change Management* 17, no. 6 (2004).

Butler, Katy. "Bouncing Back: The Anatomy of Resilience, New Research Reveals What Helps People Shake Off Adversity," *Family Therapy Networker* (March/April 1997): 22–31.

Croft, Lucy and Natasha Cochrane. "Communicating change effectively," *Management Services* 49, no. 1 (Spring 2005).

DiGeorgio, Richard. "Winning with Your Strengths: An Interview with Ken Tucker of the Gallop Organization," *Journal of Change Management* 4, no. 1 (Mar 2004): 75–81.

Diggins, Cliona. "Emotional intelligence: The Key to Effective Performance," *Management International Digest* 12, no. 1 (2004).

Easterbrook, Gregg. "The Real Truth about Money," *Time* vol. 165, 155.3 (Jan 17, 2005): A 32.

Ebberwein Christopher A.; Thomas S Krieshok; Ellie C. Prosser; Jon C. Ulven. "Voices in Transition: Lessons on Career Adaptability," *The Career Development Quarterly* 52, no. 4 (Je 2004): 292–308.

Folaron, Jim. "The Human Side of Change Leadership," *Quality Progress* 38, no. 4 (Apr 2005).

Fredrickson, Barbara L. "The Value of Positive Emotions," *American Scientist* (July/Aug. 2003): 330–335.

Hathaway, Patti, CSP. "When You're at the End of Your Rope, Let Go!" www.thechangeagent.com.

McCarthy, Bill. "The Two Dimensions of Organizational Change," *Strategic HR Review* 4, no. 1 (Nov/Dec 2004).

Morgan, Timothy. "Purpose Driven in Rwanda," *Christianity Today* (October 2005).

Morris, Holly J. "Happiness Explained," *U.S.News & World Report* (Sept 3, 2001): 46.

O'Neil, William J. *Military and Political Leaders & Success,* New York: McGraw-Hill 2005.

Pearsall, Paul. "The Beethoven Factor: The People That Thrive in the Face of Adversity May Surprise You," *Psychotherapy Networker* (Jan./Feb. 2004,): 56–61.

Prochaska, J. O., and W. F. Velicer. "The Transtheoretical Model of Health Behavior Change," *American Journal of Health Promotion* (1997).

Putz, Michael, and Michael E. Raynor. "CEO Advisory: Integral Leadership: Overcoming the Paradox of Growth," *Strategy & Leadership* 33, no. 1 (2005).

Richardson, John H. "Whee! (A Special Report from the Happiness Project)," Research by Ed Diener. *Esquire*, vol. 137 iss. 6 (June 2002): 82–5.

Scott, Arlene. "Leading Change," *Leadership Excellence* 22, no. 3 (Mar 2005).

Sheler, Jeffery. "Preacher with a Purpose," *U.S.News & World Report* (October 2005). www.usnews.com.

Vakola, Maria, Ioannis Tsausis, and Ioannis Nikolau. "The Role of Emotional Intelligence and Personality Variables on Attitudes Toward Organisational Change," *Journal of Managerial Psychology* 19, no. 1/2 (2004): 88–110.

Wallis, Claudia. "The New Science of Happiness: What Makes the Human Heart Sing?" *Time*, vol. 165, iss. 3 (Jan 17, 2005): A2.

Wiseman, Richard. "Lucky People," *Skeptical Inquirer* (May/June 2003): 26–30.

Wiseman, Richard. The Luck Project. www.luckfactor.co.uk.

Zoroya, Gregg. "One wild ride for jackpot winner," *USA Today*. www.usatoday.com.

Website References
www.ehealthmd.com (Dictionary)
http://wordnet.princeton.edu/perl/webwn (Dictionary)
www.elisabethkublerross.com/ (Stages of Grief)
www.noogenesis.com/malama/discouragement/helplessness.html (Learned Helplessness)
www.uncommon-knowledge.co.uk/goal_setting/smart_4.html (SMART Goals)

INDEX